Battleground Europe

ST JULIEN

Graham Keech

Series editor
Nigel Cave

LEO COOPER

First published in 2001 by
LEO COOPER
an imprint of
Pen & Sword Books Limited
47 Church Street, Barnsley, South Yorkshire S70 2AS

Copyright © Graham Keech, 2001

ISBN 0 85052 839 9

A CIP catalogue of this book is available
from the British Library

Printed by CPI UK

For up-to-date information on other titles produced under the Leo Cooper imprint,
please telephone or write to:
Pen & Sword Books Ltd, FREEPOST, 47 Church Street
Barnsley, South Yorkshire S70 2AS
Telephone 01226 734222

Battleground Europe
ST JULIEN

Other guides in the Battleground Europe Series:

Walking the Salient *by* Paul Reed
Ypres - Sanctuary Wood and Hooge *by* Nigel Cave
Ypres - Hill 60 *by* Nigel Cave
Ypres - Messines Ridge *by* Peter Oldham
Ypres - Polygon Wood *by* Nigel Cave
Ypres - Passchendaele *by* Nigel Cave
Ypres - Airfields and Airmen *by* Michael O'Connor
Ypres - St Julien *by* Graham Keech

Walking the Somme *by* Paul Reed
Somme - Gommecourt *by* Nigel Cave
Somme - Serre *by* Jack Horsfall & Nigel Cave
Somme - Beaumont Hamel *by* Nigel Cave
Somme - Thiepval *by* Michael Stedman
Somme - La Boisselle *by* Michael Stedman
Somme - Fricourt *by* Michael Stedman
Somme - Carnoy-Montauban *by* Graham Maddocks
Somme - Pozieres *by* Graham Keech
Somme - Courcelette *by* Paul Reed
Somme - Boom Ravine *by* Trevor Pidgeon
Somme - Mametz Wood *by* Michael Renshaw
Somme - Delville Wood *by* Nigel Cave
Somme - Advance to Victory (North) 1918 *by* Michael Stedman
Somme - Flers *by* Trevor Pidgeon
Somme - Bazentin Ridge *by* Edward Hancock

Arras - Vimy Ridge *by* Nigel Cave
Arras - Gavrelle *by* Trevor Tasker and Kyle Tallett
Arras - Bullecourt *by* Graham Keech
Arras - Monchy le Preux *by* Colin Fox

Hindenburg Line *by* Peter Oldham
Hindenburg Line Epehy *by* Bill Mitchinson
Hindenburg Line Riqueval *by* Bill Mitchinson
Hindenburg Line Villers-Plouich *by* Bill Mitchinson
Hindenburg Line - Cambrai *by* Jack Horsfall & Nigel Cave
Hindenburg Line - Saint Quentin *by* Helen McPhail and Philip Guest

La Bassée - Neuve Chapelle *by* Geoffrey Bridger

Mons *by* Jack Horsfall and Nigel Cave
Accrington Pals Trail *by* William Turner
Poets at War: Wilfred Owen *by* Helen McPhail and Philip Guest
Poets at War: Edmund Blunden *by* Helen McPhail and Philip Guest
Poets at War: Sassoon & Graves *by* Helen McPhail and Philip Guest

Gallipoli *by* Nigel Steel

Italy - Asiago *by* Francis Mackay

Boer War - The Relief of Ladysmith *by* Lewis Childs
Boer War - The Siege of Ladysmith *by* Lewis Childs
Boer War - Kimberley *by* Lewis Childs
Isandlwana *by* Ian Knight and Ian Castle
Rorkes Drift *by* Ian Knight and Ian Castle

Hougoumont *by* Julian Paget and Derek Saunders

WW2 **Pegasus Bridge/Merville Battery** *by* Carl Shilleto
WW2 **Utah Beach** *by* Carl Shilleto
WW2 **Gold Beach** *by* Christopher Dunphie & Garry Johnson
WW2 **Omaha Beach** *by* Tim Kilvert-Jones
WW2 **Sword Beach** *by* Tim Kilvert-Jones
WW2 **Battle of the Bulge - St Vith** *by* Michael Tolhurst
WW2 **Battle of the Bulge - Bastogne** *by* Michael Tolhurst
WW2 **Dunkirk** *by* Patrick Wilson
WW2 **Calais** *by* Jon Cooksey
WW2 *Das Reich* – **Drive to Normandy** *by* Philip Vickers
WW2 **Hill 112** *by* Tim Saunders
WW2 **Market Garden - Nijmegen** *by* Tim Saunders
WW2 **Market Garden - Hell's Highway** *by* Tim Saunders

Battleground Europe Series guides under contract for future release:
Somme - High Wood *by* Terry Carter
Somme - German Advance 1918 *by* Michael Stedman
Somme - Combles *by* Paul Reed
Somme - Beaucourt *by* Michael Renshaw
Walking Arras *by* Paul Reed
WW2 **Boulogne** *by* Jon Cooksey
Wars of the Roses - **Wakefield/ Towton** *by* Philip A. Haigh

With the continued expansion of the Battleground series a **Battleground Series Club** has been formed to benefit the reader. The purpose of the Club is to keep members informed of new titles and to offer many other reader-benefits. Membership is free and by registering an interest you can help us predict print runs and thus assist us in maintaining the quality and prices at their present levels.

Please call the office 01226 734555, or send your name and address along with a request for more information to:
Battleground Series Club Pen & Sword Books Ltd,
47 Church Street, Barnsley, South Yorkshire S70 2AS

CONTENTS

Introduction by the Series Editor 6
Author's Introduction 8
Acknowledgements 10
Advice to Travellers 12
List of Maps 16

Chapter 1   **Autumn 1914 – Spring 1915** 17
Chapter 2   **The First Gas Attack** 30
Chapter 3   **The Second Gas Attack** 57
Chapter 4   **Reorganisation and Withdrawal** 85
Chapter 5   **Recipients of the Victoria Cross** 95
Chapter 6   **Battlefield Tours** 105
           Appendix 1 125
           Appendix 2 127
           Appendix 3 128
           Appendix 4 131
           Appendix 5 134
           Appendix 6 137

           Further Reading 141
           Selective Index 142

St Julien in 1915 partially destroyed by 'friendly fire'.

Introduction by Series Editor

It is now over thirty years since I first visited the St Julien memorial at Vancouver Crossroads. It struck me then as a powerful and evocative memorial; and in all the visits and years that have passed since, that impression has firmly remained.

The Second Battle of Ypres is remembered above all else for the first use of gas. In a world that has by now become accustomed to the barbarities of modern warfare, it is difficult for us to comprehend just how scandalised the allies were by the first use of this ghastly weapon. Contemporary accounts by all ranks express their horror and contempt. Perhaps more than any other event on the Western Front it acted as a clear cut off from whatever notions of chivalry that had existed up to that time. Gas was not used in the same way during the Second World War; a clear example of the deterrent effect that was obtained by the fact that both sides were known to have the potential to launch this particularly ghastly weapon in the horrific business of war. Ghastly

certainly; lethal – not particularly. Yet I have early memories of our next door neighbour when we lived in Crowborough; East Sussex. He had been gassed during the war, and there he was, in the 1960s, effectively confined to bed by the serious damage the gas had caused to his lungs.

Although the Canadians played a vital part in the battle, it is easy to forget the significant contribution of the French army. In fact it is difficult to find much evidence of the presence of the French army at all in the Ypres Salient – but they were there and in considerable numbers in both 1914 and 1915.

This book sets out the events of the fighting around Second Ypres in 1915 and takes the visitor to the major sites and the cemeteries and memorials that are closely linked with it. The countryside is largely unchanged in the areas beyond the vicinity of Ypres, but modern industrial (and housing) development has served to obscure or put under concrete some parts of the battlefield.

Besides a battlefield on the ground, it also caused the final falling out in the uneasy relationship between General Sir Horace Smith-Dorrien and Sir John French, resulting in the former's sacking in the middle of a battle.

The battle is a rare example of one of the few occasions when the Germans launched a major offensive action on the Western Front. It was ill-resourced to fulfil the potential that the chaos of the new weapon presented, and can be described as a failure. But it most certainly did leave the allies in a very tenuous position in the salient around Ypres, and made any subsequent attempt to break out from this position very difficult. The line that was reached by the end of the fighting was, effectively, the line from which the British started their attack over two years later, on 31st July 1917, subsequently known as the Third Battle of Ypres. The Canadians, who figure prominently in this account, were to fight battles once more, in the dying days of that battle, just to the right of where they had been in the early days of the fighting in 1915.

Nigel Cave
St Mary's, Derryswood

7

Author's Introduction

When in May 1921 the Battles Nomenclature Committee published its report it divided the Battles of Ypres, 1915, into four distinct actions. The first and second of these, the Battles of Gravenstafel and St. Julien are covered in this volume under the one heading, St. Julien. The Gravenstafel action involved the first use of asphyxiating gas as a weapon of war and the consequences of this use led directly to the second action, around St. Julien. The Battles Nomenclature Committee also defined the duration of the Gravenstafel fighting as being over the two days 22 and 23 April whilst St. Julien started on the following day, 24 April and continued until the withdrawal was completed, on 4 May. This time span also defines the period of this book.

Gas! A single word which like no other is synonymous with the horror that was the First World War. It is generally accepted that the Germans were responsible for the first use of gas, in the attack carried out on 22 April 1915. However, various unsubstantiated claims have been made for earlier uses. It seems likely that some, if not all, of these claims were mistaken. There is evidence that experiments with new and modified explosives led to the production of gases, with odours, which had not been previously experienced on fields of battle. These unknown odours were erroneously reported as being due to the deliberate release of gas rather than to being products of detonations.

If the Germans had exploited this new weapon to the full, then the whole course of the war could have been altered. Had they followed up the breakthrough, on the French front, Ypres could have fallen and the future of the BEF put in jeopardy. It is probable that, as was to happen with innovations made on the allied side, the senior commanders lacked faith in the 'new fangled ideas' and therefore did not use them as well as they might have done. It must also be pointed out that there are misconceptions about the extent to which gas was used during the remainder of the war. The release of chlorine, as cloud gas, by the Germans ceased in 1916, mainly as a result of adverse wind conditions. After this time they relied on the use of gas shells, with a variety of gas, liquid and particulate fillings. However, the British continued to use cloud gas release up to the end of the war and were poised to use it more widely still had the war continued into 1919.

The Ypres Salient is usually described, as being flat, which, is to a large extent true. However, there are a number of low ridges, **(See map 1 page 17)** which became very important features in the fighting. The largest of these ridges, the Passchendaele Ridge, runs north-eastwards

8

for some four and a half miles with others, such as the Zonnebeke Ridge, running in an east-west direction. Between the ridges there are several streams or beeks. The most important of these is the Steenbeek with its tributaries the Haanebeek and Lekkerboterbeek. In 1915 there were also several woods, the largest of which, Kitchener's Wood, no longer exists but its position has recently been marked by a memorial. An area between Gravenstafel and St. Julien, containing a length of poor trench and a few old buildings, was known as to the Canadians as 'Locality C'. Situated on the skyline, on the western part of Gravenstafel ridge, about 800 yards west of Boetleer's Farm, it became an important defensive point. At the start of the 1915 fighting many of the villages, whose names were to become so well known to the people back in England, were still inhabited and animals roamed the fields. Life was going on as it had done before the intervention of war. Ypres itself was largely intact, although the Cloth Hall and St. Martin's Cathedral displayed the scars of German bombardments in 1914. The inhabitants of Ypres preferred to stay and to guard their property, rather than to leave it to the military! In addition to the villages there were numerous farms, dotted over the landscape. One such, which features many times in the narrative, is Mouse Trap Farm, which was about half a mile north of Wieltje. Originally called Shell Trap Farm the name was changed because the authorities considered the old name to be bad for morale. By the end of 1915 many of these farms were no more than ruins. Most were rebuilt after the war but often not quite in the same location. The farms had extensive cellar networks, the ruins of which

The Cloth Hall at Ypres after the early bombardment in 1914-15.

The Cloth Hall photographed in 1918 shows the damage sustained by that year. Taylor Library

would have proved too costly to excavate in order to rebuilt on the same site. The opportunity was taken to move the farms nearer to the service roads. However, with judicious use of trench and modern maps the original sites can be located. The nomenclature used throughout the text is either that of the period or that adopted by the British Official Historian. In some cases there have been changes e.g. Ypres is now Ieper, St. Jean is now Sint Jan and St. Julien has become St. Juliaan, but each is easily recognisable.

As has happened in other theatres e.g. the Australians in Gallipoli, some actions have become associated with specific units to the exclusion of all others. Such is the case with the repulse of the enemy after the release of chlorine gas. That the Canadians played a very important role is undeniable, but many British and French troops were also involved. In the course of the story certain battalions will appear for one action and then seem to disappear without trace. Where this occurs the reader is asked to be forbearing. To account for every movement, back and forth, would inevitably lead to an almost unreadable account.

Acknowledgements

In order to write this book I have had to read numerous war diaries of the units involved. Some are very full and give graphic accounts of the events as they took place. Others are very brief and refer to the actions, in which many brave men lost their lives, as every day events.

But the modern day researcher owes a great debt to the men who, in many cases, kept meticulous records for posterity. In order to read their words access to the Public Record Office is essential. I wish to pay tribute to the work of all the men and women involved at Kew, and in particular to those in the Reading Room, Library and Map Room who helped me with my researches.

Alongside the war diaries, as sources of information are the histories, compiled soon after the end of the war, often by men who served with the particular division or battalion. I would like to thank the staff of the Reading Room at the Imperial War Museum who helped me locate many such works. At the same time I would like to thank members of the photographic archive of the same museum who helped me with contemporary photographs. I am also grateful to the Trustees of the Imperial War Museum for permission to reproduce certain of these photographs. The photographs concerned are referred to in the text by the letters IWM together with a Q reference number. I am also indebted to Andrew Whitmarsh of the Royal Air Force Museum for his help and advice on aerial photographs.

As I point out in the 'Advice to Travellers' section maps covering the St. Julien area are not easily available. I am grateful to M. Hubert Lardinois of the Belgian Institut Géographique National for his advice and help on the subject of maps.

As also mentioned in the 'Advice to Travellers' section the 'In Flanders Fields' Museum in Ypres is very impressive. I would like to thank Peter Schlosse, the Head of Tourism in Ypres for his advice and introduction to the curator of the Museum Education Department, Jan Dewilde. Through the department I was able use the Rose Coombs and Dr. Caenepeel archives. I am also very grateful to Jacky Platteeun, who I met in the museum, for his help with the pre-war pictures of St. Julien.

In the course of my researches into the role of the Green Howards I am grateful for the assistance given to me by the curator of the Regimental Museum, Richmond Yorkshire, Colonel Neil McIntosh MBE.

When visiting battlefields it is always good to have a good 'bag man' to offer advice, assistance and to read the maps. I am, therefore, grateful to Peter Wilson who accompanied me on two trips to St. Julien.

Finally, I would like to thank Peter Batchelor for our discussions on the VCs, Nigel Cave for his usual patience and advice, and last but not least, all the production staff at Pen & Sword Ltd.

Advice to Travellers

Old battlefields can still be dangerous places! When visiting any Great War site the chances are that you will see shells and other detritus of war left, on the side of the road, for collection by the authorities. Leave them there and do not be tempted to move or even touch them. Many are still live with the potential to kill or maim.

As with any trip abroad it is advisable to go with adequate insurance cover for yourself, members of your party and for your vehicle. In order to receive reciprocal medical treatment in France and Belgium be sure to take a copy of Form E 111, which can be obtained from most Post Offices. Many providers of motor insurance no longer actually issue a Green Card, to extend motor policies for foreign travel, but always check with you insurer before leaving. Most require to be given the dates of your trip together with a list of the countries to be visited. In addition do take out breakdown and recovery cover for your vehicle through the AA or RAC.

Remember there is often no cover on battlefields, so always go prepared for extremes of weather. Even in summertime the temperature can soon change and what was a sunny summer day turn

The statue of Marechal Foch in the Public Gardens.

into one of rain, often of almost monsoon proportions. For the walks stout shoes or walking boots are recommended, as the ground can be treacherous. It is also a good idea to take a picnic or snack with you so that you can maximise your time on the ground.

All the tours start from the most central point of Ypres (Ieper), the market square (Grote Markt). To reach Ypres from Calais there are several routs and the one chosen is a matter of personal preference. A particularly attractive route is to go via Cassel, which provides a good lunch stop, as there are several reasonable cafés on the old cobbled square. If time permits, visit Maréchal Foch's statue in the Public Gardens and the nearby Castel

Plaque on Hotel Schoebeque.

Yvonne, No 1 Rue St. Nicholas, which was General Plumer's headquarters. On the right hand side of the road out of Cassel, rue du Maréchal Foch, is the old Hotel de Schoebeque. On the front of the building is a plaque recording the names of numerous personalities who visited or stayed there during the Great War.

Ypres itself is a pleasant city with numerous hotels, restaurants and cafés. The first point of call should be the Tourist Office, which is located in the main square, Grote Markt, and is part of the 'In Flanders Fields' Museum located at the end of the Cloth Hall.

General Plumer's headquarters.

> 'In Flanders Fields' Museum
> Lakenhallen
> Grote Markt 34
> B – 8900 Ieper
> *Tel. (0032) 57 22 85 84*
> *Fax. (0032) 57 22 85 89*
> E-mail: flandersfields@ieper.be
> E-mail: toerisme@ieper.be

There are numerous hotels and restaurants on the square and full details may be obtained from the Tourist Office. However, the following suggestions may be helpful.

Hotels:

Ariane Hotel
Slachthuisstraat 58
B-8900 Ieper
Tel. (0032) 57 21 82 18
Fax. (0032) 57 21 87 99
E-mail: info@ariane.be
Website: www.ariane.be
Natasja Feliers

Albion Hotel
St. Jacobstraat 28
B-8900 Ieper
Tel. (0032) 57 20 02 20
Fax. (0032) 57 20 02 15
E-mail: info@albionhotel.be
Website: www.albionhotel.be
Christine Decramer-Praet

Bed & breakfast:

Camalou
Dikkebusseweg 351
B-8908 Ieper
Tel. (0032) 57 20 43 42
Fax. (0032) 57 21 78 62
E-mail: info@camalou.com
Website: www.camalou.com
Annette Linthout

Camalou is approximately 4 kilometres from the centre of Ypres, close to Dikkebus lake on the N375 road to Bailleul.

Varlet Farm
Wallenmolenstraat 43
8920 Poelkapelle
Tel. & Fax. (0032) 51 77 78 59
E-mail: varlet.farm@ping.be
Website:www.battlesfields.freeserve.co.uk/varlet1.htm
Dirk & Charlotte Carden-Deschamps

Varlet Farm is close to Poelkapelle. Once in, or near, Poelkapelle it is well signposted.

Maps

The area around Ypres is covered by four Belgian 1: 25,000 maps:
> Sheet No. 28/1-2 Poperinge-Ieper
> Sheet No. 28/3-4 Geluveld-Moorsele
> Sheet No. 20/5-6 Lo-Langemark
> Sheet No. 20/7-8 Staden-Roeslare.

However, these maps were issued in 1991 and 1977 respectively and are therefore somewhat out of date. They are also difficult to obtain, other than direct from the Institut Géographique National, Comptoir

des vents, Abbaye de la Cambre 5, B-1050 Bruxelles Belgium.
E-mail: sales@ngi.be

The best alternative is the French IGN 1: 100,000 Green Series Map No. 2, Lille-Dunkerque, which covers Ypres. In addition the Michelin 1:200,000 No. 51 overprinted with the Commonwealth War Cemeteries and Memorials is very useful. The latter can be obtained from the Commonwealth War Graves Commission at the addresses below. Finally, trench maps will be found to be of value although they are not available for the period of the fighting covered by this volume. However, those for 1917 give many of the locations mentioned in the text and are therefore useful. Members of the Western Front Association can obtain such maps from the Association and in addition there is now a CD-ROM, 'The Imperial War Museum Trench Map Archive', produced by the Naval and Military Press which includes St. Julien. The address for the Naval & Military Press is also given below.

Commonwealth War Graves Commission
Head Office
Commonwealth War Graves Commission
2 Marlow Road
Maidenhead
Berks SL6 7DX
Tel. 01628 634 221
E-mail: general.enq@cwgc.org

Northern Europe Area
Commonwealth War Graves Commission
Elverdingsestraat
B-8900 Ieper
Belgium
Tel. (0032) 57 20 01 18
E-mail: neaoffice@cwgc.org

Naval & Military Press
The Naval & Military Press
Unit 10
Ridgewood Industrial Park
Uckfield
East Sussex
TN22 5QE
Tel. 01825 749 494
E-mail: order.dept@naval-military-press.co.uk
Website:www.great-war-trench-maps.com

List of Maps

1. Ypres 1915. Farms and ridges. (Based on map in PRO CAB 45/155). 1
2. Ypres 1915. French & Belgian sectors. (Based on Official History Map). 1
3. Ypres 1915. The British sector. (Based on Official History Map). 2
4. Ypres 1915. The G.H.Q. Line. (Based on Official History map). 2
5. Ypres 1915. The German dispositions. 22 April. (Based on Official History Map). 2
6. Ypres 1915. British & French dispositions. 22 April. (Based on Official History Map). 3
7. Ypres 1915. First gas attack. (Based on Official History Map). 3
8. German Front Line. Midnight 22 April 1915. (Based on Official History Map). 4
9. Canadian attack. Midnight 22 April 1915. (Based on Official History Map). 4
10. Geddes's Detachment. (Based on Official History Map). 5
11. British attack. 4.15 p.m. 23 April 1915. (Based on Official History Map). 5
12. Second gas attack. (Based on Official History Map). 5
13. Lahore Division attack. 26 April 1915. (Based on Trench Map). 7
14. Lahore Division attack. 27 April 1915. (Based on Trench Map). 7
15. Plumer's new line. 3 May 1915. (Based on Official History Map). 8
16. Approximate locations of Victoria Cross winners. (Based on *Canada in Flanders* Map). 9
17. Battlefield Car Tour No. 1. (Based on *Canada in Flanders* Map). 104
18. Battlefield Car Tour No. 2. (Based on *Canada in Flanders* Map). 11
19. Battlefield Walk No. 1. (Based on Trench Map). 117
20. Battlefield Walk No. 2. (Based on Trench Map). 12

Chapter One

AUTUMN 1914 – SPRING 1915

The First Battle of Ypres officially ended on 22 November 1914. The British Expeditionary Force, the BEF, had suffered in the region of 60,000 casualties of which 2,500 were officers. These losses, together with those suffered at Mons, on the Aisne and in the period prior to 'First Ypres' meant that the old British Army had been severely tested.

With the Old Army almost gone and the New Army not yet ready, the last month of 1914 and the early months of 1915 were times of intense anxiety for the British High Command. The BEF was short of

Map 1: Ypres 1915. Farms and Ridges.

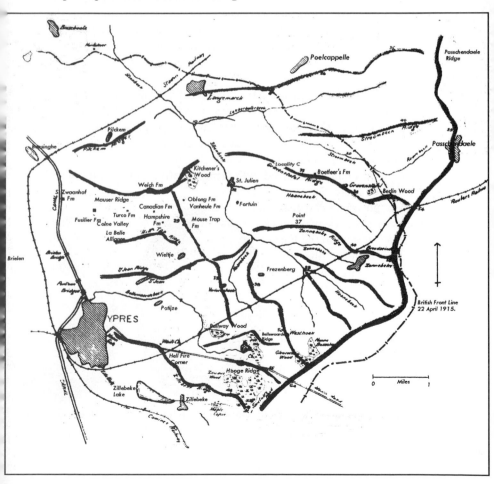

regular soldiers and of the materiel of war. High explosive shells, in particular, were in such short supply that the artillery was only permitted to expend a handful of shells per gun per day. Indeed, the supply of artillery pieces (and in particular the right type) and shells was to remain a problem well into 1916.

In late November it became clear that the enemy was reducing his strength on various parts of the front, in Belgium and France, in order to bolster his numbers in the East. General Joffre, eager to exploit the perceived weaknesses, urged the British Commander-in-Chief, Sir John French, to join in a combined Anglo-French offensive in mid-December. The resulting attacks and the German counter-attacks achieved little, other than to increase still further the British casualty figures, particularly in the 7th Division.

By mid-December practically all the Army Reservists and pre-war Special Reserves had been utilised. More than twenty Territorial Force battalions and six Yeomanry Regiments were in France with others due to arrive by the turn of the year. The time had come to reorganise. On 25 December an order was published to the effect that, as from noon on 26 December, two armies would be created. The First Army, commanded by General Sir Douglas Haig, to consist of I Corps, IV Corps and the Indian Corps whilst the Second Army, commanded by General Sir Horace Smith-Dorrien, was to be made up of II Corps, III Corps and the 27th Division. The Cavalry Corps and the Indian Cavalry Corps were to be commanded by Lieutenant-General Sir E H Allenby and Major-General M F Rimington respectively.

Sir John French conferred with General Joffre, at Chantilly, on 27 December. Here, he expressed the British government's fears for the consequences of a quick German success in the East. London believed that the release of large numbers of troops and their redeployment in the West would adversely affect the ability of the allies to withstand attacks in France and Belgium. Ideas for actions in other theatres were already beginning to circulate but Sir John

Field-Marshal Sir John French.   **General Joffre.**

French and General Joffre both felt that the war could only be won in the West. Consequently, while the Germans adopted a purely defensive attitude in France and Belgium the staffs at St. Omer, the British GHQ, and at Chantilly, the French GQG, began to prepare elaborate plans for a 1915 offensive as soon as weather and ground conditions would allow.

With a view to threatening the long enemy lines of communication, General Joffre expressed his wish to mount French attacks in Champagne, on the Artois plateau and on the Verdun-Nancy front. Sir John French,whilst eager to co-operate with General Joffre, at the same time wished to improve his own front line positions. By early January 1915 the line held by the BEF ran from Cuinchy in the south to St. Eloi in the north. The southern sector was held by the First Army and the remainder, from Bois Grenier northwards, by the Second Army. In front of the former, in the waterlogged Lys valley, lay the drier ground of the Aubers Ridge. Besides better trench conditions, the ridge would give excellent views towards Lille and its important rail systems.

Map 2: Ypres 1915. French and Belgian sectors.

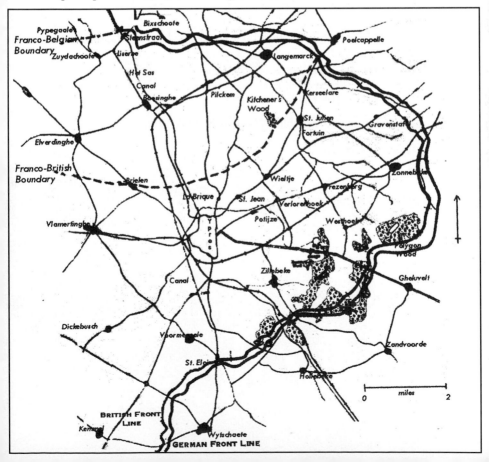

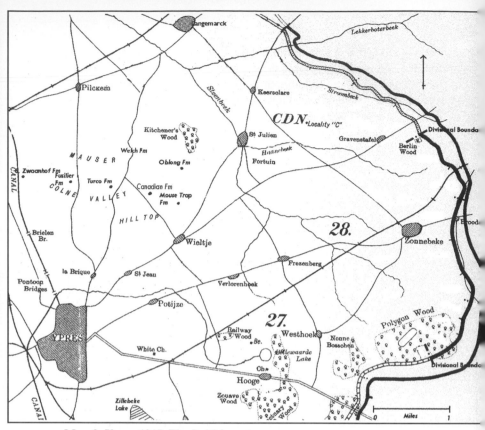

Map 3: Ypres 1915. The British sector.

Canadian troops on Salisbury Plain, September 1914. IWM Q 53259

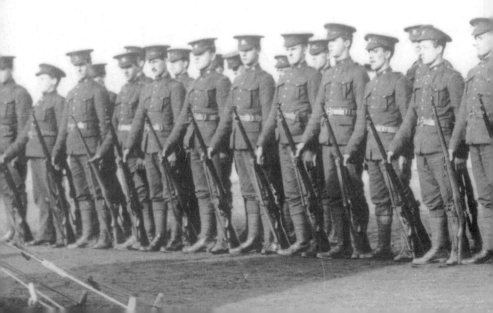

General Joffre agreed that an attack in this area would co-ordinate well with his projected attack by the French Tenth Army in the vicinity of Arras but before the French could launch their attacks, General Joffre insisted that British troops should relieve the French IX and XX Corps north of Ypres. Sir John French, who expected the 29th Division and the 1st Canadian Division to reach France in February, readily agreed to these changes. Subsequently, General Joffre modified his request suggesting instead that only IX Corps be relieved, allowing it to join in the attack by the French Tenth Army. When Sir John French learned that the 29th Division was no longer available (it went to Gallipoli), he considered its replacement, the 46th (North Midland Territorial Division) insufficiently trained to go directly to the front. The Canadians had already been earmarked to join in the First Army offensive and so he felt that he could no longer fulfil his commitment to relieve the French IX Corps. On 7 March, General Joffre informed Sir John French that, given the Field-Marshal's inability to relieve IX Corps, he would be forced to postpone his own attacks. Sir John French was determined to proceed with the plans laid by the First Army and the Battle of Neuve Chapelle was fought between 10 and 13 March.

Negotiations between the two commanders were resumed on 24 March, when General Joffre again requested the immediate relief of the IX and XX Corps with a view to launching a combined offensive at the end of April. On 1 April Sir John French responded by ordering an extension of the British line by almost five miles, to the Ypres-Poelcappelle road beyond Zonnebeke, the move to be completed by 20 April. At the same time he expressed a hope that he would be in a

Ontario Royal Artillery on parade.

position for the First Army to join in an offensive. The movements sanctioned by Sir John French involved transferring the Canadian 1st Division to the Second Army where, together with the British 27th and 28th Divisions, it made up the recently formed V Corps **(See appendix 1)**. Lieutenant-General Sir HCO Plumer, commanding V Corps, was made responsible for the new sector where, between 2 and 17 April, the Corps replaced three French divisions. These changes made the Second Army responsible for two-thirds of the Ypres Salient and left the French defending the northern flank. Their line extended westwards for five miles from the Ypres-Poelcappelle road to the Yser canal at Steenstraat. It was manned by two divisions: the 45th (Algerian), on the right and the 87th (Territorial) on the left. These two divisions, together with a detachment of cavalry, constituted the Groupement d'Elverdinghe commanded by General Quiquandon, which in turn, with the Groupement de Nieuport, made up the French Détachement d'Armée de Belgique commanded by General Putz **(See appendix 2)**. The Belgian Army held the line from Steenstraat northwards to Nieuport where the French were once more in control **(See map 2 page 19)**.

Lieutenant-General Sir HCO Plumer

From the Ypres-Poelcappelle road the Second Army line was held on the left by the Canadians, in the centre by the 28th Division and on the right by the 27th Division **(See map 3 page 20)**. The front taken over from the French consisted, for the most part, of isolated breastworks rather than formal trenches. A continuous trench system could not be dug due to the presence of water very close to the surface. The parapets were generally quite thin and were not bullet proof; there were no paradoses. The only communication trenches ran between the

22

front and support lines. Much work had to be done by the British troops, to render the positions secure, when they took over the lines. Major H H Mathews of the 8th Battalion (Winnipeg Rifles) CEF. described his entry into the trenches in a long report:

The 2nd Brigade was ordered to take over its line, from the French, on the night of Wednesday 14th April, and motor buses were again provided, this time for all the troops, taking us during the afternoon through Poperinghe and on to Vlamertinghe about three miles east of Ypres.

It was curious sight to see the long line of buses with their loads of soldiers (25 to a bus) winding along the road, the journey was accomplished without a hitch, and very materially helped out what would otherwise have been a long and tiresome march.

The parapet was very poor, the wire entanglements in places extremely weak and sanitary arrangements of the most primitive order. We busied ourselves as well as we could during the day and first night remedying these defects.

At dusk guides were sent out to bring in the relieving company of the Buffs, but the night was wet and inky black which caused considerable delay; during this time we managed to repair the damage done to the parapet during the day.

Early in the morning Private Ingalls had been killed, he had carelessly exposed his head over the parapet. This was the first man we had had killed in the Company, and the funeral in the pitch dark night and rain and solemn words of the Chaplain, Captain Woods, impressed me very much. But I must admit that later, during the hard days of fighting that followed, one became very callous and indifferent.[1]

Private Ingalls has no known grave but is commemorated on the Menin Gate Memorial.

French troops being transported in London Buses.

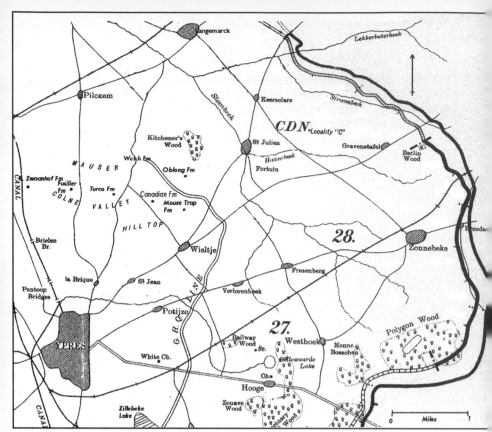

Map 4: Ypres 1915. the G.H.Q. Line.

The difficulties encountered by the French, in constructing a proper trench system led them to design what became known, to the British, as the 'GHQ Line' **(See map 4)**. It ran from Zillebeke Lake, where it was a mile or so behind the front, northwards to a point half a mile east of Wieltje, where it was three miles behind the front. Thence it gradually turned north-westwards to join a line covering Boesinghe village and railway bridge. Unlike the front line this reserve line was well constructed. It consisted of a series of redoubts, four to five hundred yards apart, each capable of holding about fifty men. In turn, these were eventually linked by a series of fire trenches. The line was well sited on forward and reverse slopes, but was in no place overlooked due to the flatness of the ground.

Four army corps held the German line in the Ypres Salient, with the distance between the two front lines everywhere between one hundred and fifty and three hundred yards **(See map 5 page 25)**. In the north, opposite the junction of the Belgian 6th Division, on the west bank of the canal at Steenstraat, and the French 87th Territorial Division on the

24

east bank, was XXIII Reserve Corps with the 45th and 46th Reserve Divisions in the line. Next, in front of the remainder of the 87th Territorial Division, the French 45th Algerian Division and part of the Canadian 1st Division, was XXVI Reserve Corps. The 52nd Reserve Division held the line opposite the 87th Territorials while the 51st Reserve Division and the attached 2nd Ersatz Brigade continued it up to the junction with XXVII Reserve Corps. This Corps had the attached 38th Landwehr Brigade opposite the Canadians near Gravenstafel, and the 53rd Reserve Division and the 54th Reserve Division opposite the British 28th and 27th Divisions respectively. Finally, XV Corps carried the line south-westwards with the 39th Division and 30th Divisions opposite the remainder of the British 27th Division and the British 5th Division. These four corps, with XXII Reserve Corps (less the 43rd Reserve Division) along the Yser and the

Map 5: Ypres 1915. German dispositions. 22 April.

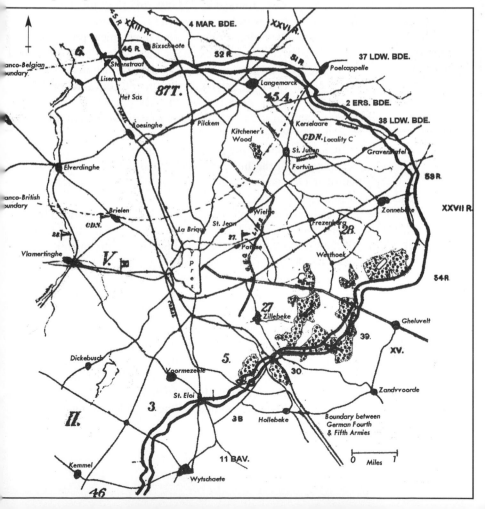

Marine Division guarding the coast, together with the Guard Cavalry Division, the 43rd Reserve Division, the 4th Ersatz Division and the 37th Landwehr Brigade in reserve, constituted the German Fourth Army commanded by General-Colonel Duke Albrecht of Württemberg **(See appendix 3)**.

Unfortunately, as was to happen at other times in the war, before the proposed allied attack could be launched the Germans struck. At 5 p.m. on 22 April, XXVI Reserve Corps attacked in the Poelcappelle–Steenstraat sector using gas, on the Western Front, for the first time.* Before dealing with the fighting which followed, the Second Battle of Ypres, it will be of interest to consider whether the British should have expected, and been prepared for, such an attack.

At the beginning of the twentieth century the German chemical industry was pre-eminent. It was particularly strong in the manufacture of dyestuffs and synthetic replacements for expensive and imported, naturally occurring, raw materials. Many of the substances, subsequently used in gas warfare, were readily available in large quantities. They were either already being used in chemical processes or could easily be derived from substances that were. One of the leading chemists was Fritz Haber, who had already contributed to the war machine when, in 1908, he solved the problem of the fixation of nitrogen, which had eluded other researchers. By this discovery the essential element required in the manufacture of explosives was made available from the air. When war broke out he made himself, and his research facilities, available to the government and remained involved with chemical warfare at the highest level for the duration. That this was the situation in Germany must have been well known to the British chemical establishment.

The use of poisonous and asphyxiating gases had been forbidden by the Hague conventions on the Laws and Customs of War. A special Hague declaration in 1899 forbade the use of projectiles the sole object of which was the diffusion of asphyxiating gases. This was later extended to cover the use of such substances in shells. It was made clear that, in such circumstances, the destructive effect of the projectile had to be greater than the deleterious effect of the gas. The 1907 convention clearly forbade the use of poison or poisonous weapons. The Germans were to state that their use of cloud gas in 1915 was within these guidelines. They argued that the gas used, chlorine, was not poisonous but merely asphyxiating and therefore its use was legitimate. They also asserted that the British had used gas shells before 22 April 1915, an accusation that had been made as long ago as

---

*There are unsubstantiated reports of earlier use on the Eastern Front.

1899-1902, by the Boers in South Africa. In fact, the smells detected had in all cases resulted from the use of picric acid in the explosive.

On 15 April General Smith-Dorrien, commander of the Second Army, forwarded to GHQ a copy of a report brought in by his liaison officer with the French commander, General Putz.

Reliable agent of the Detachment of French Army in Belgium reports that an attack round Ypres has been arranged for night 15/16 April. A prisoner of 234th Regt. XXVI Corps, taken on 14th April near Langemarck, reports that an attack has been prepared since noon 13th. Reserves have been brought up and passages have been prepared across old trenches, existing in rear of present German trenches, to facilitate bringing forward artillery. Germans intend making use of tubes with asphyxiating gas placed in batteries of 20 tubes for every 40 metres on front of XXVI Corps.

The prisoner had in his possession a small sack filled with a kind of gauze or cotton waste which would be dipped in some solution to counteract the effects of the gas. German moral is said to have much improved lately owing to having been told that there is not much in front of them.

It is possible that if the wind is not favourable, and so it blows the gas over own trenches, that the attack may be postponed.[2]

Unfortunately, General Putz entered a caveat with the report. He added that, on interrogation, the prisoner seemed to be so knowledgeable that it was likely that he had been sent over to deceive. Nevertheless the following day No. 6 Squadron of the Royal Flying Corps was ordered to investigate the German lines, but reported nothing unusual. Nor was this the first indication that the French had had of a possible attack with asphyxiating gas. Prisoners taken on the German XV Corps front near Zillebeke, at the end of March, had given similar information when questioned. Although reported to the Tenth Army no further action was taken.

Also on the 15th, V Corps intelligence sent the information, supplied by the prisoner, to all divisions. In fact he was a driver who had deserted and surrendered to the French 4th Battalion of Chasseurs. In 1930 the French General Ferry, who commanded the French 11th Division from 1914 to April 1915, published a magazine article in which he named the deserter as one August Jaeger. The unfortunate

General Sir H Smith-Dorrien.

Jaeger was arrested, charged with desertion and betrayal, and sentenced to ten years by a German court.

On 16 April a further report was circulated by the French Army giving details of information received, by the Belgian Army, from a reliable agent:

> The Germans have had made in Ghent, on a rush order, 20,000 mouth protectors of Tulle, which the soldiers will carry in a waterproof cloth bag 10cm by 17.5cm. The mouth protectors, soaked in a suitable liquid, will serve to protect the men against the heavy asphyxiating gas which the Germans intend to discharge towards the enemy lines, notably on the front of the XXVI Reserve Corps. The men of that corps have recently received at Roulers, special instruction to learn the handling of gas cylinders; these last will be placed on the ground to the extent of one battery of 20 cylinders every 40 metres.[3]

On 17 April a German wireless communiqué reported that the British had 'yesterday, east of Ypres, used shells and bombs with asphyxiating gases'. This untrue report was designed to justify the use of such gases by the Germans in the near future.

It would be both unfair and untrue to say that no action was taken in response to the intelligence. On 15 April, 28th Division issued Operation Order No. 30, which referred to 'reliable information having been received that the enemy have arranged to attack the Ypres Salient to-night'. It went on to give orders for actions to be taken to counter the attack. This order was followed up the next day by V Corps Operation Order No. 11, signed by Brigadier-General H S Jeudwine, which directed the 27th and 28th Divisions to select places of assembly

A group of Germans demonstrate their gas masks for the camera.

in anticipation of the town of Ypres having to be evacuated. There was no mention of action to be taken by the 1st Canadian Division since, at that time, it was not yet responsible for any part of the line. The order made it clear that it was being issued because of certain information that had been communicated to Divisional Commanders. In this final sentence may lie the answer to the question: why were we not better prepared? It would seem likely that the possibility of a gas attack was taken seriously at corps and divisional levels but that the concern was not passed down to brigades and battalions. The British Official Historian does however, refer to the war diary of the Assistant Director of Medical Services (A.D.M.S.) of the 1st Canadian Division, who records the mention of the possibility of a gas attack at a meeting on 15 April. Brigadier Edmonds adds that, here is no confirmation of this discussion in other war diaries.

In defence of the inaction it has been stated that the senior officers could not believe that the German High Command would ever sanction an action which they considered to be in breach of the accepted laws and usages of civilised warfare. At a later time in the conflict they would almost certainly not have put forward this view. Where serious consideration was given to a possible gas attack, it was believed that the area over which such an attack could be launched would necessarily be small. This being the case it was felt that an immediate counter-attack, as was prescribed in the event of a mine explosion, would drive the enemy from any ground gained.

After the war, German sources confirmed that their original intention had been to release gas on the sector occupied by their XV Corps, between the Ypres-Comines Canal and the Menin road. The breadth of the front had later been extended to cover Zillebeke, as stated by one of the prisoners. They also confirmed that the cylinders had been dug in and were ready for use from late February onwards. That no attack had taken place was due to adverse weather conditions, particularly the direction of the wind. Eventually on 25 March, the order was given to change the point of attack to the front of XXVI Reserve Corps, between Poelcappelle and Steenstraat. Preparations were completed by early April and the attack was set for 15th of the month, confirming the intelligence given by August Jaeger. Postponement was again necessitated by the lack of a favourable wind.

Bibliography
1. Public Record Office. CAB 45/156.
2. War Diary II Army. General Staff. Public Record Office. WO 95/270.
3. *Official History of the Canadian Forces in the Great War 1914-1919*. Volume I. Col. A. F. Duguid. Ottawa. 1938.
4. *Military Operations in France & Belgium*. 1915. Volume I. Edmonds. Macmillan. 1927.

Chapter Two

THE FIRST GAS ATTACK

By 22 April, the changes to the British positions, agreed by Sir John French at the beginning of the month, had been completed. Lieutenant-General Sir Herbert Plumer, commanding V Corps, with his headquarters in Poperinghe, seven miles west of Ypres, had three divisions in the line. From the junction with the French on the Poelcappelle road to the boundary with the 28th Division at Berlin Wood, the 1st Canadian Division held the line, commanded by Lieutenant-General E A H Alderson, with headquarters in the Chateau

Map 6. Ypres 1915. British and French dispositions. 22 April.

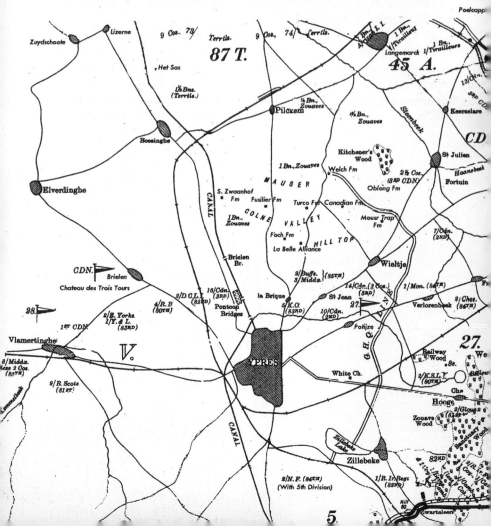

Chateau des Trois Tours, Canadian headquarters 1915. IWM Q 56710

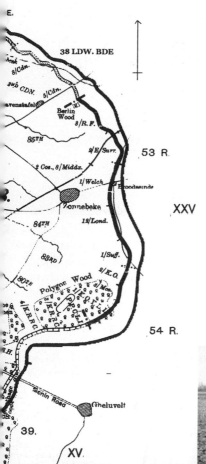

des Trois Tours, near Brielen. The Division had the 3rd Brigade on the left and the 2nd Brigade on the right facing units of the German XXVI and XXVII Reserve Corps. The 3rd Brigade had two battalions, the 13th and 15th, in the line and one battalion, the 14th, in reserve in St. Jean. The 2nd Brigade also had two battalions, the 8th and the 5th, in the line and one battalion, the 7th, in reserve at St. Julien. The remaining two battalions were in divisional reserve, on either side of the canal. The 16th was near a temporary bridge at Brielen and the 10th between St. Jean and Ypres. The 1st Brigade was in army reserve, at Vlamertinghe, nearly three miles west of Ypres **(See map 6)**.

From Berlin Wood down to

Berlin Wood.

Potijze Chateau, May 15. IWM Q 512119

Polygon Wood the 28th Division, Major-General E S Bulfin, held the line, with from left to right the 85th, 84th and 83rd Brigades. These brigades had three, three and two and a half battalions respectively in the line. In brigade reserve were two battalions near Verlorenhoek; and in divisional reserve, three battalions near St. Jean and two and half battalions west of Ypres. The Divisional headquarters was in Vlamertinghe chateau.

Finally, the 27th Division, Major-General T D'O Snow (headquarters at Potijze), occupied the sector from the centre of

Polygon Wood almost to Hill 60. Southwards, from its junction with the 28th Division, each of its three brigades: the 80th, the 81st and the 82nd, had three battalions in the front line; with two battalions in support in and behind Sanctuary Wood; in divisional reserve were two battalions north-west of Ypres and one near Vlamertinghe.

The original German plan envisaged using gas to break into the north-eastern shoulder of the Salient, then to push forward along the line of the Yser Canal to effect the capture of Ypres. The latter was to be part of a larger offensive to roll up the whole Salient. However, General von Falkenhayn, Chief of the German General Staff, would not provide the additional troops required for this ambitious plan. As a consequence, the scheme set down on 8 April had as its objective the Pilckem ridge and the ground adjoining it to the east. On the 14th, this plan was updated to include specified objectives for the units involved. Thus, the 45th Reserve Division would capture Steenstraat, the 46th Reserve Division would secure the line of the Yser Canal with bridgeheads at Het Sas and Boesinghe, and both divisions would co-operate in the capture of Lizerne. The first objective of XXVI Reserve Corps would be the line of high ground following the road between Boesinghe and Poelcappelle through Pilckem and Langemarck **(See map 1 page 17)**. Finally, the 52nd Reserve Division was made responsible

Map 7: Ypres 1915. First gas attack 5 p.m., 22nd April.

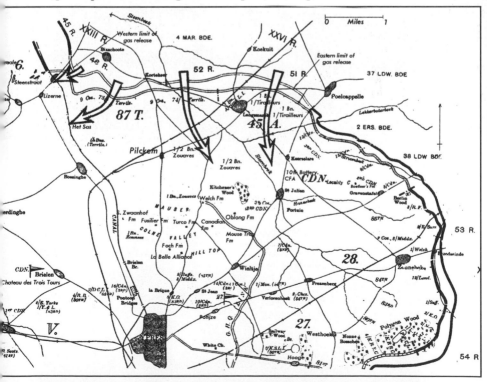

for the capture of Pilckem, while Langemarck was left to the 51st Reserve Division.

Almost 6,000 cylinders of chlorine gas – a total of 149,000kg – had been dug into the front line, ready for release. The cylinders were grouped in batteries of ten, connected by a manifold to a single discharge pipe. This pipe was then led over the parapet, held down by sandbags, and directed towards the French lines. Chlorine is a gas, which is heavier than air, has a greenish-yellow colour and is classed as a lung irritant. It causes irritation of the conjunctiva and the mucous membranes of the nose, larynx and pharynx. In sufficient concentration it becomes lethal.*

In preparation for their attack on 22 April the Germans opened up a bombardment, three days before, on the 19th. When dawn broke on the 22nd there was little or no wind. In fact it was to be a glorious spring day. The Canadians, in spite of having been working hard all night

*A quantity of cylinders had been placed on Hill 60. Fearful of their discovery, the Germans made repeated attempts to retake the hill following its capture, by the British, on 17 April. They finally succeeded on 5 May.

Germans lay out pipelines before a gas attack. TAYLOR LIBRARY

Royal Engineer's sketch of method used to release asphyxiating gas. PRO WO 95/744

improving their trenches, were set to withstand an early morning attack, but none developed. The gas attack had been scheduled for 5.45 a.m., but fifteen minutes before zero hour the order was cancelled, due to lack of wind. The bombardment however continued, fire being mainly concentrated on trenches, roads and bridges; but the villages, and the town of Ypres did not escape. Among the shells fired were a number containing the lachrymatory gas T-Stoff, a mixture of xylyl and benzyl bromides. As the day progressed the fire eased somewhat but, at 5.00 p.m., heavy and concerted shelling of Ypres and of the nearby villages recommenced. At the same time heavy fire was laid down on the French forward trenches. The valves on the chlorine cylinders were opened for five minutes, and propelled by a breeze blowing at about five miles per hour, the first cloud gas attack of the war was launched, against the French 45th Algerian Division. The infantry units were ordered to advance 15 minutes after the gas **(See map 7 page 33)**.

Observers on the Canadian front became aware of two clouds, one either side of Langemarck, moving across the French lines. The clouds hugged the ground, and still moving in the direction of Ypres, soon merged into one long bank of greenish-yellow fog. The smell of the gas was detected as far as five miles behind the front line, but the maximum effect was experienced in an area bounded by Steenstraat, Boesinghe, Keerselare and the German line north of Langemarck. Within minutes terrified French African infantrymen were streaming back from the front, with eyes streaming, coughing and fighting for breath. The gas attack was seen by several senior British officers: by General Smith-Dorrien, who was returning on foot to Ypres, after visiting Hill 60, by Major-General Snow commanding the 27th Division from his headquarters in Potijze; and by Lieutenant-General Alderson, who was visiting Canadian artillery units near St. Julien.

In his despatch to the Secretary of State for war Lord Kitchener, dated 15 June 1915, Sir John French was to

Lieutenant-General E A H Alderson

35

Lieutenant-General Alderson with members of the Canadian 1st Division Staff.

make the following comment on the use of gas:

> I much regret that during the period under report the fighting has been characterised on the enemy's side by a cynical and barbarous disregard of the well-known usages of civilised war and flagrant defiance of the Hague convention.
>
> All the scientific resources of Germany have apparently been brought into play to produce a gas of so virulent and poisonous a nature that any human being brought into contact with it is first paralysed and then meets with a lingering and agonising death.
>
> The enemy has invariably preceded, prepared and supported his attacks by a discharge in stupendous volume of these poisonous fumes whenever the wind was favourable. Such weather conditions have only prevailed to any extent in the neighbourhood of Ypres, and there can be no doubt that the effect of these poisonous fumes materially influenced the operations in that theatre, until experience suggested effective counter-measures, which have since been perfected to render them innocuous.
>
> The brain power and thought which has evidently been at work before this unworthy method of making war reached the pitch of efficiency which has been demonstrated in its practice shows how the Germans have harboured these designs for a long time.

Chlorine gas sweeping over trench lines.

> *As a soldier I cannot help expressing the deepest regret and*
> *some surprise that an Army which has hitherto claimed to be the*
> *chief exponent of the chivalry of war should have stooped to*
> *employ such devices against brave and gallant foes.*[1]

The opening of the attack was followed by a period of intense activity,
at battalion, brigade, division and army levels. The early responses
often resulted from receipt of false reports and it was not until about
11 p.m. that any degree of clarity and order was established. The
commanding officer of the Canadian 3rd Brigade, Brigadier-General R
E W Turner, whose 13th and 15th Battalions were closest to the French,
ordered up his reserve battalion, the 14th, from its position at St. Jean,
to his headquarters at Mouse Trap Farm. The reserve units of the in line
battalions, in St. Julien, were also moved to cover the village.
Meanwhile as the bulk of the French units fled back, away from the
front, one battalion of 1/1st Tirailleurs, unaffected by the gas, remained
in position, along with two support half battalions of 1/2nd Zouaves.
The commander of the company on the left of the 13th Battalion led
one of his platoons across the Poelcappelle road to join up with the
Tirailleurs. Forced by the lack of cover in the French trench to seek a
better position, they spread out in echelon and along the ditch in front
of the Poelcappelle road, where another platoon and a machine gun
unit joined them. Seven hundred yards behind, also in the ditch, were
two support platoons but, from there on, there existed a gap of some
two thousand yards. When the 14th Battalion arrived at Mouse Trap
Farm it deployed northwards past the farm and in the GHQ Line above

Casualties of the first gas attack in a French trench near Langemarck,

the Wieltje-St. Julien road. Here they were joined by about 500 Zouaves, who extended to the left by Hampshire Farm. The German efforts to advance were finally stopped by guns of the 10th Battery, Canadian Field Artillery. The Canadian artillery had been ordered to assist the French. The 10th, commanded by Major W B King, was in an orchard, 500 yards north of St. Julien and a hundred east of the road to Keerselare. They watched in horror as the French streamed back and were themselves severely affected by the gas but at 5.45 p.m. they opened fire on the enemy front line. At 7.00 p.m. a mass of Germans were seen some 200 or 300 yards away moving south, in what had been French territory. Major King reversed one section and opened fire. The Germans immediately took cover and started to dig in. Realising that his position was precarious Major King called for infantry backup. Sixty men of the 14th and 15th Battalions were sent from St. Julien, under the command of Lieutenant G W Stairs.* (Amongst the party was Corporal F Fisher of the 13th Battalion, in charge of a machine-gun. For his actions that day Corporal Fisher was awarded the Victoria Cross **(See chapter 5)**.

At Canadian Divisional headquarters Lieutenant-General Alderson received reports that: the front was wide open; the French had

*Lieutenant Stairs was killed two days later. His name appears on the Menin Gate Memorial.

French Zouaves overcome by gas.

collapsed; and St Julien was now in the Canadian front line. In response he placed one of his divisional reserve battalions, the 16th, under the command of Brigadier-General Turner and ordered a second, the 10th, to report to Brigadier-General Turner as soon as possible. Unfortunately, in trying to carry out this order, the 10th Battalion was held up by congestion on the roads and was forced to take up a temporary position in the GHQ Line south and south-east of Wieltje.

Both Canadian Brigades were made aware of the necessity of holding on and not allowing any breaks to occur in their lines. In command of the 2nd Brigade, Brigadier-General A W Currie received a request at 7.00 p.m. for support from Brigadier-General Turner. He immediately ordered up his brigade reserve, the 7th Battalion, and deployed it; half at Spree Farm, near the cross roads 1,000 yards south-east of St. Julien, and half at the cross roads south of Locality C, known as Bombarded Cross Roads. Later it moved to Locality C on the skyline on the western part of Gravenstafel ridge, about eight hundred yards west of Boetleer's Farm.

Canadian artillery with 4.7 inch gun.

Newspaper propaganda picture of German soldier's protection against British gas shells.

Second Army headquarters first received news of the attack, via V Corps, at about 6.45 p.m. Mistaken reports, augmented by inaccurate messages from General Putz, led General Smith-Dorrien to fear for the safety of all the troops and guns to the east of Ypres. In an effort to restore the line he moved, from the Army reserve, the Canadian 1st Brigade and placed it under V Corps and at the same time ordered the 2/East Yorkshire, in 28th Division reserve, to Lieutenant-General Alderson's command at Brielen. The Battalion's Commanding Officer was given specific orders to watch the situation along the canal in case the Germans broke through at Het Sas or Steenstraat or attempted to cross nearer to Ypres. Lieutenant-General Plumer, in command of V Corps, immediately released two battalions of the Canadian brigade, the 2nd and 3rd, to Lieutenant-General Alderson, who sent them to the assistance of the 3rd Brigade.

As the evening progressed General Smith-Dorrien became more and more convinced that the French had to be induced to attempt a restoration of their line. Representations to General Foch led to an infantry regiment and additional artillery, from General Putz's reserve, being allocated to General Quiquandon (French 45th Division), who then proposed to carry out a counter-attack at 4.30 a.m. on the following morning. It was agreed that British troops on the new flank would co-operate in this attack under the command of Lieutenant-General Alderson.

In reality the situation, in the early evening, was that the Canadian line was intact. Two platoons of the 13th Battalion lined the ditch of the Poelcappelle road in support of the 1/1st Tirailleurs. The latter still held about 100 yards of their original trench with the enemy some 150 yards away. About six hundred yards in the rear, and also deployed along the ditch, were two supporting platoons of the 13th Battalion and a few Algerians who had rallied there. Then there was a gap of 1,700 yards to the orchard where the 10th Battery was in action supported by men of the 14th and 15th Battalions. Southwest of St. Julien and above the Wieltje road was one company of the 7th Battalion, which had become detached from the remainder of the battalion. Another gap extended 1,000 yards to the GHQ Line where a mixture of engineers, Zouaves and three companies of the 14th Battalion extended past Mouse Trap Farm to Hampshire Farm, where they were in touch with the enemy 400 yards to the north. Westwards to the Canal de l'Yser, 3,000 yards, was a gap unoccupied save for one French machine-gun post discovered at 9.30 p.m. to be in contact with the German firing line on Mauser ridge.

The distance between the enemy on Mauser Ridge and the British front line at Hill 60 was less than four miles. If the Germans had pressed their attack they might well have cut off as many as 50,000 troops together with 150 guns. In their path lay only three reserve battalions of the 28th Division: the 5/King's Own, the 2/Buffs and 3/Middlesex, which were in St. Jean when the attack was launched.

British and French prisoners, captured on 22 April, awaiting trnnsport.

When the fleeing Algerians were seen by the commanding officer of the Middlesex, Lieutenant-Colonel E W R Stephenson, he ordered his own battalion and the 2/Buffs to deploy on a 2,000 yard front along the ridge covering the villages of St Jean and La Brique. The line extended down to the canal at bridge No. 2, 1,000 yards north of Ypres. The 5/King's Own remained in reserve to this new line. The line ran at right angles to the Canadian 16th Battalion on the canal bank, near the Brielen Bridge. Also in the vicinity of this bridge was the 2nd Field Company Canadian Engineers, at Burnt Farm, who on seeing the stream of gassed French troops, began setting charges to blow up the bridges over the canal. One party went up to bridge, No 5; a second to bridge No 4, the Brielen Bridge, whilst a third wired up Nos. 3, 3A and 2. Later in the evening men of the 1st Field Company set charges on the remaining two bridges, No.1 and A.

At 7.55 p.m. Brigadier-General Currie received a second request for aid, from the 3rd Canadian Brigade:

Brigadier-General Currie.

We have no troops between C.22.b (Brigade H.Q. Mouse Trap Farm) and St. Julien.

Can you occupy this line? Please reply.

Signed G. B. Hughes Lieut.-Col.[2]

It was on receipt of this request that Brigadier-General Currie moved what he thought was the whole of his 7th Battalion to Locality C to protect his own front line. From his remaining reserves, he sent a machine-gun section and a grenade company to Brigadier-General Turner, but retained two infantry battalions.

In the 27th Division General Snow, on becoming aware of the attack reacted immediately without waiting for orders from V Corps. He moved the 4/Rifle Brigade from divisional reserve to a position between Potijze and St. Jean, and split the 2/King Shropshire Light Infantry (KSLI) between divisional headquarters at Potijze and the 80th Brigade headquarters at Verlorenhoek. On the 28th Division front, Lieutenant-Colonel Stephenson's deployment of the 2/Buffs, the 3/Middlesex and the 5/King's Own was followed by orders to the 1/York & Lancaster to reinforce St. Jean. As the regiment

Lieutenant-Colonel E W R Stephenson

was some way west of Ypres it did not arrive until the next morning, by which time all four battalions had been placed at the disposal of the Canadian Division. One half of the 3/Middlesex, under the command of Major G H Neale, was sent to secure the Brielen Bridge, where it replaced the 2nd Canadian Field Company. Finally, to provide a local reserve, General Bulfin ordered his last two reserve battalions, the 2/Cheshire and the 1/Monmouthshire, to a position under the Frezenberg ridge.

Shortly before 9.00 p.m. the Germans launched an attack directed at the 1/1st Tirailleurs, at the junction with the Canadians. At first the Tirailleurs were forced back but eventually, with the aid of men from the 13th Battalion, managed to halt the advance and set up a new defence line along the Poelcappelle road. Here they were joined by one company of the 2/Buffs, under Captain F W Tomlinson, which had been sent forward by Colonel Geddes at the request of Brigadier-General Turner. At daybreak the original line was re-established.

Brigadier-General Turner received news of General Quiquandon's proposed counter-attack towards Pilckem at about 9.00 p.m., along with a request for support.

As soon as you get your two battalions together make a counter-attack towards the wood C.10 d. (Kitchener's Wood) and

Map 8: German Front Line. Midnight 22 April 1915.

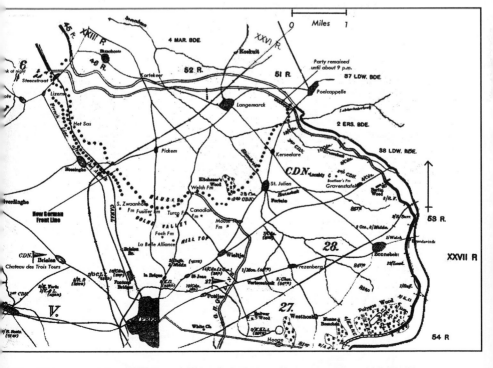

*then on towards U 27.(Area between Pilckem and Langemarck)
The French are counter-attacking towards PILCKEM. A
battalion of the 28th Div. (1/York & Lancaster) is coming to your
support.*

> *From Canadian 1st Division*
> *G W Gordon-Hall, Lt.-Col.*[3]

Before examining the first major counter-attack it will be instructive to
look at the exact position of the German line just before midnight on
22 April **(See map 8 page 43)**. As already recorded, the objectives for
the German attack included Steenstraat, Lizerne, Het Sas, Pilckem, the
line of the ridge marked by the road, Boesinghe-Pilckem-Langemarck.
For some unknown reason the gas release opposite Steenstraat was
limited and the village did not fall to the 45th Reserve Division until
late evening. The 46th Reserve Division crossed the canal; it took Het
Sas but was stopped east of Boesinghe. Almost as soon as the release
of gas was stopped the 52nd Reserve Division rushed forward to
capture Pilckem. Although subsequently ordered not to press on
beyond the southern slope of the ridge, by the time the order was
received, the leading troops were already close to the canal. They took
up positions on Mauser Ridge, in Kitchener's Wood and on the road
over the Steenbeek south-west of Langemarck. In these positions they
were reinforced by the 37th Landwehr Brigade, which established a

Map 9: Canadian attack. Midnight 22 April 1915..

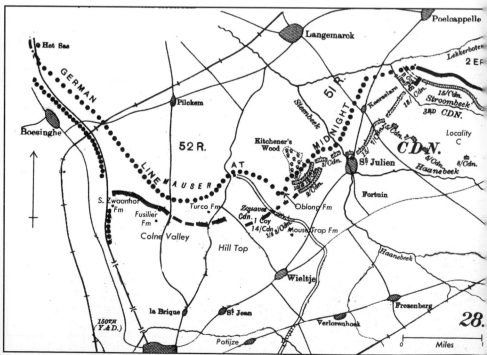

28.

second line along the Pilckem ridge. Finally, the 51st Reserve Division easily captured Langemarck, moved south-eastwards parallel with the line of the Langemarck-Keerselare road, to a position in front of the Keerselare-St. Julien road.

The two battalions referred to in the order from the Canadian 1st Division above were the 10th and 16th. When Brigadier-General Turner issued the order for the attack, at 9.40 p.m., the 16th was still on its way up from Brielen:

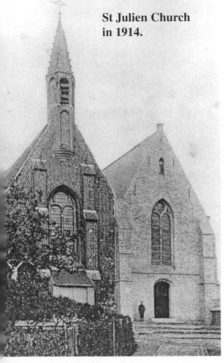

St Julien Church in 1914.

10th and 16th Bns. in that order will counter-attack at 11.30 p.m. Bns. will assemble in C.23.a, north of GHQ Line. Clear wood C.10.d. Direction N.W. to U.27. Attack on frontage of two companies. Remaining six companies in close support at 30 yards distance on same frontage. Artillery shell C.5.c. (i.e. 400 yards N. of Kitchener's Wood) and N.W. of that square [4]

The assembly position was set at 500 yards north-east of Mouse Trap Farm **(See map 9 page 44)**. The 10th Battalion (Lieutenant-Colonel R L Boyle) was in the van with the 16th Battalion

St Julien Church, already badly damaged, in early 1915.

(Lieutenant-Colonel R G E Leckie) in the rear. Observers, watching the enemy lines before nightfall, had seen intense activity in and around Oblong Farm. Lieutenant-Colonel Boyle was fearful of machine-gun fire from this direction; a fear which was to prove fully justified. He considered whether he should sent troops to deal with the farm but on re-reading his orders decided that it was not his responsibility and would be dealt with by others. At 11.48 p.m. the order was given to advance, with covering fire from only three batteries - all the remaining artillery was in the process of moving to more secure positions - the Canadians started down the slope towards the objective.

Not a sound was audible down the long lines but the soft pad of feet and the knock of bayonet scabbards against thighs.[5]

Half way to the wood the leading units ran into a wired hedge and, as they forced their way through, the enemy opened fire. Many men fell: after a momentary delay, the fence yielded and the hoards rushed the German trench and were into the wood. After fierce hand to hand fighting the remnants of the 10th Battalion reached the northern edge of the wood and started to dig in. Meanwhile the 16th swung to the right and exited from the wood and along the north-eastern edge.

Messages were sent back to the Canadian Division reporting the success but stating that contact had not been made with the French. The Canadians now found themselves under fire from the rear and when Major D M Ormond, adjutant of the 10th, went to investigate he discovered a German redoubt in the south-western extremity of the wood, close to the captured trench. He set about organising an attack on the redoubt but its firepower was so great that he was forced to withdraw. By now the state of the Canadians was perilous. Two-thirds of the officers, all the company commanders and half of the men of the 10th had already fallen. Among the wounded was Lieutenant-Colonel Boyle, who had been hit five times in his left thigh:

The grave of Lieutenant-Colonel Boyle in Poperinghe Old Military Cemetery.

Battalion stretcher-bearers dressed the colonel's wounds and carried him back to the battalion first aid station. From there he was moved to Vlamertinghe Field Hospital,

46

13th Field Ambulance at Vlamertinghe. The first gassed Canadians from the action at St Julien were taken here after receiving primary attention at the field dressing station.

and from there to Poperinghe. He was unconscious when he reached hospital, and died shortly afterwards without regaining consciousness.

Major J MacLaren, the second-in-command, was also wounded. He and another officer were transported back to a dressing station in the rear of a staff car. When the driver reached the station and opened the door he found his passengers dead. A shell had apparently passed through the vehicle and decapitated both men.

The 16th Battalion had fared little better. It had lost fifty percent of its strength, including its adjutant and three company commanders.

But the surprises for the Canadians were not over. They discovered that the enemy still occupied a large area in the north-west part of the wood and a trench running westwards from the south-west corner. While the counter-attack was in progress the 2nd and 3rd Battalions, released by General Plumer, had arrived at Mouse Trap Farm. The 2nd Battalion (Lieutenant-Colonel D Watson) sent in one company, to reinforce the attack on the left, but as it moved forward the early morning mist suddenly lifted, exposing it to the German machine-gunners who took a heavy toll. The situation was now deemed to be untenable and so orders were sent to evacuate the forward positions.

The new line was established along the southern edge of the wood. At 5.00 a.m. it was extended to the right, in the direction of St. Julien, by half of Lieutenant-Colonel R Rennie's 3rd Battalion.

Among those who saw the attack was Canon Frederick Scott, who recalled the scene:

Aerial photograph of St. Julien battlefield in 1917. IWM Q 43220

*The battalion rose and fixed bayonets and stood ready for the
command to charge. It was a thrilling moment, for we were in the
midst of one of the decisive battles of the war. A shrapnel burst
just as the men moved off and a man dropped in the rear rank...
It was an awful and wonderful time. Our field batteries never
slackened their fire and the wood echoed back the crackling*

> *sound of the guns. The flare-lights all round gave a lurid background to the scene. At the foot of the long slope, down which the brave lads had gone to the attack, I saw the black outline of the trees. Over all fell the soft light of the moon. A great storm of emotion swept through me and I prayed for our men in that awful charge, for I knew that the Angel of Death was passing over our lines that night'* [7]

As already noted, at 12.30 a.m., the four battalions: 2/Buffs, the 3/Middlesex, the 5/King's Own and 1/York & Lancaster were placed at the disposal of the Canadian Division.* Lieutenant-General Alderson put these units under the command of the senior officer, Colonel A D Geddes of the 2/Buffs, to form the Geddes's Detachment. At about 2.00 a.m. Captain Crichton arrived with orders for Colonel Geddes and to act as his Staff Officer. As a consequence of the orders the 2/Buffs (Major R E Power) was detailed to advance, via Wieltje, to connect with the 3rd Canadian Brigade, which was endeavouring to establish itself in front of Kitchener's Wood. On making contact it was to extend to the left. The 3/Middlesex was to advance on the left to connect with the French and then extend to the right whilst the 5/King's Own (Lieutenant-Colonel Lord R F Cavendish) was to advance up the

* Less two companies of 3/Middlesex and one company 2/Buffs.

Map 10: Geddes's Detachment.

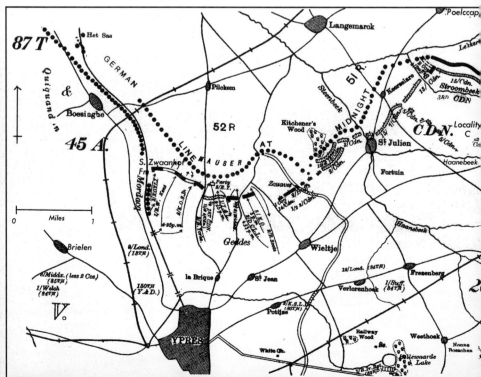

Pilckem road and connect up with the other two battalions. Finally, the 1/York & Lancaster was to follow the 5/King's Own in reserve. Meanwhile Colonel Geddes established his headquarters at Wieltje **(See map 10 page 50)**.

The advance was carried out under fire but by 9.30 a.m. a practically continuous line was established between the 3rd Canadian Brigade, at Kitchener's Wood, and the 1st Canadian Brigade on the canal. That this was possible was due to the introduction of the Canadian 1st Brigade and other French and British units into the line. Ordered to support the French counter-attack, Brigadier-General M S Mercer

Brigadier-General M S Mercer

(1st Canadian Brigade) sent the 1st Battalion (Colonel F W Hill) and the 4th Battalion (Lieutenant-Colonel A P Birchall) from Brielen to a position adjacent to the Pilckem road, where they linked up with the 3/Middlesex. At 6.45 a.m. Colonel Mordacq (90th Brigade, 45th Division), in charge of the French operations on the east bank, sent a party of Zouaves to link up with the Canadian 1st Brigade near the canal. The projected French counter-attack was postponed until 3.00 p.m. to permit additional artillery to be brought to bear. This delay also gave time for two battalions of the 27th Division, 2/DCLI (Lieutenant-Colonel H D Tuson) and 9/Royal Scots (Lieutenant-Colonel A S Blair), to be added to Geddes's command, along with the 2/East Yorkshire from 28th Division.

Whilst preparations for the afternoon attack were being laid, a meeting at Cassel was convened between Sir John French and General Foch. Sir John agreed to co-operate in the attempt to retake the ground lost by the French but at the same time expressed concern for the situation in the Salient. On returning to his headquarters, at Hazebrouck, Sir John increased the strength of the Second Army by placing the three infantry battalions of the 50th Division under General Smith-Dorrien's command. Two of these, the 150th and 151st, were sent to the 28th Division, while the third the 149th, was ordered to a position between Poperinghe and Vlamertinghe. Later in the day the 1st Cavalry Division arrived in the area and orders were sent from the Commander-in-Chief that two brigades of the 4th Division, and the Lahore Division of the Indian Corps, should be readied to move northwards. Shortly after the arrival of the

Maréchal Foch.

Cavalry Division the 13th Brigade (Brigadier-General R Wanless O'Gowan) joined them.

Orders were issued for an attack between Kitchener's Wood and the canal at 3.00 p.m. Brigadier-General Wanless O'Gowan commanded the operation directed at Pilckem. Delays in getting troops into position led to the start being put back to 4.15 p.m. but, even so, no time was available for thorough preparation and reconnaissance. Colonel Geddes did not receive the orders placing him under the command of Wanless O'Gowan and so acted independently. General Putz ordered the 45th Division to attack east of the canal with the British, while the remainder of his force continued to fight at Lizerne and Steenstraat. In the event the only involvement of the 45th Division was a minor attack near the canal by about 400 Zouaves. The more northerly attacks met with little success

Such was the ground – open, with little cover and sloping up towards the enemy lines – that the attack had little chance of success. On the right, under Lieutenant-Colonel Tuson, was the 2/DCLI, supported, on its right, by two companies of the 9/Royal Scots **(See map 11)**. In the centre, required to pass through two Canadian battalions, were the 2/East Yorkshire and 1/York & Lancaster, with the 5/King's Own in reserve. These central battalions were under the command of Colonel Geddes. On the left the 1/Royal West Kent and 2/KOSB were supported

Map 11: British attack at 4.15p.m., 23 April 1915.

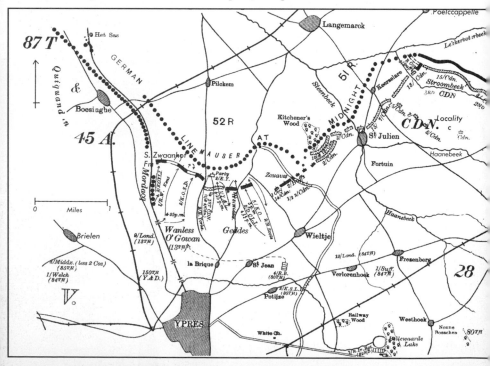

by the 2/KOYLI and the 9/London (Queen Victoria's Rifles) under Wanless O'Gowan himself. On a bright spring afternoon the ranks of soldiers, as they rose from the ground, presented wonderful targets to the German rifles and machine-guns. The enemy immediately opened up intense fire and few got within 200 yards of the enemy positions. There was some hand-to-hand fighting in the farms and cottages used by the Germans as advance positions but by 7.00 p.m. all fighting had stopped. The 3/Middlesex, and the 1st and 4th Canadian Battalions, not supposed to be involved, joined in as the attack developed. The British Official Historian recorded:

> Sir John French's promise to General Foch had been redeemed, the attack had been a magnificent display of discipline and courage: the offensive at all costs carried to an extreme. It certainly had the effect of stopping the enemy's advance in this quarter, but the price paid had been very heavy, and actually no ground was gained that could not have been secured, probably without any casualties, by a simple advance after dark, to which the openness of the country lent itself. It is obvious now that it was a mistake to agree to whatever General Joffre's deputy wished, without regard to British ideas. [8]

The cost to the units involved was very high:

> The 1/York & Lancaster lost its commanding officer, Lieutenant-Colonel A G Burt, killed, 13 officers and 411 other ranks; the 2/East Yorkshire, 14 officers and 369 men (it was reduced to 7 officers and 280 men); the 2/KOSB, 2/Duke of Cornwall's LI and 5/King's Own between 200 and 300 each; the 1st and 4th Canadian Battalions lost, respectively, 11 officers and 393 other ranks, and 18 officers (including Lieutenant-Colonel A P Birchall,

Lieutenant-Colonel Burt.

The death of Lieutenant-Colonel Birchall leading the 4th Canadian Battalion.

killed) and 436 other ranks. Lieutenant-Colonel E W R
Stephenson of the Middlesex was killed, and only twenty men of
his two companies remained: it was the end of the half battalion. [9]
Under cover of darkness the British line was adjusted and consolidated.
The new line ran from Kitchener's wood to Hampshire Farm across
Colne Valley and on to the junction with the French in front of South
Zwaanhof Farm. The two Canadian battalions and the remnants of the
3/Middlesex went into 13th Brigade reserve and the 4/Rifle Brigade
was directed to the 13th Brigade from the 27th Division, at a point near
the Brielen Bridge. Still very worried about the situation east of the
canal, where there were almost no French troops, General Smith-
Dorrien was delighted to learn that he was being sent reinforcements in
the form of the 10th Brigade (Brigadier-General C P A Hull) and that
reserves were also be pushed up to the French. However, these did not
help with the situation at the apex of the Salient. Here the Canadian
13th Battalion and the 2/Buffs were forced to withdraw, in the early
evening, to link up with the Canadian 7th Battalion:

> *In the course of the afternoon the battalion received an order*
> *to make its position secure that night. At half-past four Colonel*
> *Hart-McHarg, a lawyer from Vancouver, Major Odlum and*
> *Lieutenant Mathewson, of the Canadian Engineers, went out to*
> *reconnoitre the ground and decide upon the position of the new*
> *trenches to be dug under the cover of darkness. The exact*
> *location of the German troops immediately opposed to their*
> *position was not known to them. The reconnoitring party moved*
> *down the slope to the wrecked houses and shattered walls of*
> *Keerselare – a distance of about 300 yards - in broad*
> *daylight without drawing a shot; but, when they looked*
> *through a window in the rear wall of one of the ruins,*
> *they saw masses of Germans lining hedges not 100*
> *yards away, watching them intently. As the three*
> *Canadian officers were now much nearer the*
> *German line than their own, they turned and*
> *began to retire at the double. They were followed*
> *by a burst of rapid fire the moment they cleared the*
> *shelter of the ruins. They instantly threw themselves*
> *flat on the ground. Colonel Hart-McHarg and*
> *Major Odlum rolled into a shell-hole near by, and*
> *Lieutenant Mathewson took cover in a ditch close*
> *at hand. It was then that Major Odlum learned*
> *that his Commanding Officer was seriously*

**Lieutenant-Colonel
W F R Hart-McHarg.**

wounded. Major Odlum raced up the hill under fire in search of surgical aid, leaving Lieutenant Mathewson with the wounded officer. He found Captain George Gibson, medical officer of the 7th Battalion, who, accompanied by Sergt. J Dryden, went down to the shell–hole immediately. Captain Gibson and the sergeant reached the cramped shelter in safety in the face of heavy fire, and there dressed the wound. They remained with him until after dark, when the stretcher-bearers arrived and carried him back to battalion headquarters; but the devotion and heroism of his friends could not save his life. The day after he passed away in a hospital at Poperinghe.[10]

Colonel Hart-McHarg is buried in Poperinghe Old Military Cemetery **(See appendix 6)**.

The command of the 7th battalion passed to Major V W Odlum.

During the night of 23/24 April V Corps learned of the situation on the French and Belgian fronts. Against the French the enemy had made little progress. He still held bridgeheads over the canal at Steenstraat and Het Sas together with a stretch of ground in between as far as the western edge of Lizerne. General Quiquandon stated that he felt confident of holding even if he had to fall back to the line of the canal. Meanwhile, the Belgian army, buoyed up by the arrival of reinforcements, had extended its line from the canal to cover Lizerne. However, this position on the west bank of the canal was in danger once Lizerne fell to the German XXIII Reserve Corps after midnight. At 3 a.m. this corps renewed its attack in an effort to turn the Belgian flank. The line held: the attackers were themselves outflanked and the Belgians linked up with the French. In turn, the French under General Codet counter-attacked at both Lizerne and Het Sas on the 24th. He drew a tight net around Lizerne but made no progress at Het Sas.

Bibliography

1. *The Despatches of Lord French. Chapman & Hall. London.* 1917.
2. *Official History of the Canadian Forces in the Great War 1914-1919.* Volume I. Col. A. F. Duguid. Ottawa 1938. Appendix. 362
3. Ibid. Appendix. 375.
4. Ibid. Appendix. 388.
5. *War Diary Canadian 10th Battalion.* Public Record Office. WO 95/3370.
6. *Canada in Flanders.* M. Aitken. Hodder & Stoughton. London. 1916.
7. *The Great War as I Saw it.* Canon F.G. Scott. Clarke & Stuart. Vancouver. 1934.
8. *Military Operations France & Belgium.* 1915 Volume 1. Edmonds. Macmillan 1927.
9. Ibid.
10. *Canada in Flanders.* M. Aitken. Hodder & Stoughton. London. 1916.

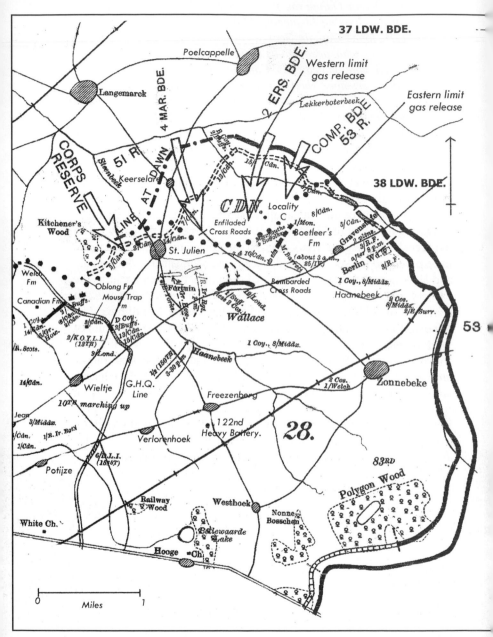

Map 12: Second gas attack 3.30 a.m. 24 April.

Chapter Three

THE SECOND GAS ATTACK

For the Canadian troops the night of 23/24 April was one of hard work. New trenches were dug, old ones repaired and lines consolidated. It was expected that another German attack was imminent but exactly where it would fall was a mystery. It was possible that attacks could be launched on any part of the Salient and could be either concerted or sequential. In fact the plan was to build upon the capture of Lizerne. The Germans intended to seize Boesinghe and then to cut off the line of retreat, at Vlamertinghe, by an encircling movement from the north. The right of the XXVI Reserve Corps would stand fast on the line from Mauser Ridge to the canal, while the 51st Reserve Division would attack the Canadian apex from three sides and advance through St. Julien and Fortuin to occupy the Zonnebeke Ridge. For this operation the thirteen battalions of the 51st Reserve Division were supplemented by the twelve battalions of the 2nd Reserve Ersatz Brigade and the 4th Marine Brigade. The XXVII Reserve Corps would join in later as the XXVI Reserve Corps moved southwards.

At 3.30 a.m. three rockets; two red and one green, rose into the sky above the Canadian lines. On the front of the 8th and 15th Battalions a cloud of chlorine gas, about a thousand yards wide, moved slowly across

A squad of German soldiers, headed by a non-commissioned officer march through a village in Flanders to the front line trenches.

No Man's Land, accompanied by a fierce bombardment **(See map 12 page 56)**. In preparation for such an attack, cans of water had been placed in the front lines, with supplies of cotton wadding, which the men were instructed to soak and hold to their faces if gas were released. This elementary form of protection saved many lives. Ten minutes later the German infantry advanced:

> *The right company of the 8th Battalion raked the approaching lines with rifle and machine-gun fire; the men of the centre and left companies, protected to some extent by the improvised respirators, helped and encouraged by the accurate shrapnel barrage, grasped their rifles and gasping yet undaunted dragged themselves dizzily up onto the battered parapet to shoot down the steadily advancing grey figures. Rifle bolts jammed,(boot heels and entrenching tool handles opened some of them. ...Platoons next to the 8th Battalion met the full potency of the gas; it penetrated what wet handkerchiefs they had, blinded all eyes with tears and filled lungs as if with cotton batting. Within the cloud, shouted orders died on frothing lips, arm signals were unseen at ten yards.*[1]

Major Mathews also recorded the effect of the gas on the 8th Battalion:

> *This wall of vapour appeared to me to be at least fifteen feet in height, white on top, the remainder being of a greenish yellow colour.*
>
> *Although the breeze was of the lightest it advanced with great rapidity and was on us in less that three minutes. It is impossible for me to give a real idea of the terror and horror spread among us all by this filthy loathsome pestilence. Not, I think, the fear of*

Early gas precautions in St Julien.

death or anything supernatural but the great dread that we could not stand the fearful suffocation sufficiently to be each in our proper places and able to resist to the uttermost the attack which we felt sure must follow, and so hang on at all costs to the trench that we had been ordered to hold.

I can truthfully say there was not a single officer or man who did not do his duty by manfully fighting down to the best of his ability the awful choking sensation and trying to stick to his post.

Many of course were absolutely overcome and collapsed on the ground, but the majority succeeded in manning the parapet as determinedly as their physical condition would permit.

They did this to such good effect that, as the fumes cleared away, an attempt to attack our left was met by so rapid a machine-gun and rifle fire that fifty or sixty Germans were killed and the attack absolutely collapsed.

They were really too easily beaten off, the men wanted to kill and go on killing, and it was hard to prevent them climbing out of the trench and making an attack on the enemy. When the fumes were fully on us breathing became most difficult, it was hard to resist the temptation to tear away the damp rags from our mouths in the struggle for air. The trench presented a weird spectacle, men were coughing, spitting, crying and grovelling on the ground and trying to be sick.

I don't suppose the worst of it lasted more than ten minutes, but we could not have stood it much longer.

After the excitement was over the symptoms, chiefly noted, were coldness of the hands and feet and great weakness, the lungs seeming to refuse to do their duty.

When I saw the men's bayonets they looked as though they had been dipped in a solution of copper. It is possible to realise to some extent what effect on human beings would be. Many of the men lay down at once and went into a deep sleep. Very few were fit for sentry duty but those that were bravely stuck to their posts, the majority of them gradually recovered and were fairly fit again by noon. The worst cases, however, were just as bad twelve hours after, and it was very difficult to get them back from the trench, the least exertion bringing on choking fits almost like convulsions.

Many of the physically strongest men were more affected than their apparently weaker comrades.

Our appetites were completely gone and hardly anyone managed to eat breakfast.

The men who gave way to the gas most easily suffered more in proportion, as unlike smoke or ordinary vapour this beastly gas seemed to be heavier than air and settled to the ground all the time, leaving a fine sediment on everything in its wake. Consequently anyone lying on the ground would be much more seriously affected than others standing up or manning the parapet. It was owing to my having to be continually on the move exhorting the men to stick to it that I got off as lightly as I did.[2]

A simultaneous attack on the north-western face of the apex was carried out without the release of gas. Due to the direction of the wind, the gas released against the 8th and 15th Battalions drifted behind, and parallel with, the lines of the 2/Buffs, and the 13th, 7th and 14th Canadian Infantry Battalions. Short of reserves, as news of the gas attack filtered back, Brigadier-General Turner had no alternative but to recall the 10th and 16th Battalions and to order the 2nd Battalion to replace them. Led by Major Ormond, the remnants of the 10th Battalion made its way from Kitchener's Wood up to Locality C, where it joined up with the 7th Battalion. At 5.30 a.m. Major Ormond received a message from Lieutenant-Colonel L Lipsett of the 8th Battalion:

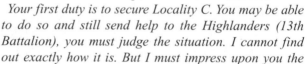

Brigadier-General R E W Turner.

Your first duty is to secure Locality C. You may be able to do so and still send help to the Highlanders (13th Battalion), you must judge the situation. I cannot find out exactly how it is. But I must impress upon you the necessity of our not allowing the Germans into Locality C.[3]

That Lieutenant-Colonel Lipsett could send such an order to Major Ormond was consequent upon the fact that Brigadier-General Currie had made him responsible for holding Locality C.

Meanwhile the 16th Battalion took up a position in the GHQ Line after a not uneventful relief. The diary of an unnamed officer is quoted in the battalion history:

All was quiet until 'stand to'; then, while it was barely daylight, a message came down from the left, that the battalion was to be relived by the 2nd. The front line was very crowded; the men from the support trench, which we had dug close behind, had moved into it. We passed the message along and waited. Daylight was coming fast; we began to wonder how we could be relieved. Somebody shouted, 'the 10th are relieved'. I looked to the left and saw, in the sort of half-light, some fellows going back over the fields behind us.

It was now broad daylight and how we were to get out was difficult to understand. We supposed it was intended that we should make a run for it over the open, and we were getting ready for the attempt when instructions came along to pass down to the right in front of the 2nd Battalion, which we did. A call came up for me from Captain Rae. I edged down the trench until I reached him. He was standing in the trench where the road cut through it. He told me that the 16th men in our section of trench were to cross the road into the ditch on the other side of it and, by means of that cover, to make their way back. My duty was to send the men across one at a time. Rae shot across. He was fired at and missed. One by one the others followed like rabbits ferreted out of their holes to be shot at. The bullets kicked up the dust every time a man got into the open. Two were hit, one in the groin, who lay on the road in great pain.

A Company Sergeant Major of the 2nd Battalion came up; his name was Winterbotham. We had a chat. He said he could give us covering fire; and a good job too, the enemy had brought up a machine-gun. There were by this time only three of us left. I

A German machine-gun team with their MG08 weapon. Taylor Library

sent over the other two, Winterbotham shook hands, and said
'Good Luck' shouted 'Go' and I went, and got safely over.[4]

On the 8th Battalion front the effect of the gas, although significant, was not sufficient to prevent the Canadians from holding back the enemy. The same was almost true for the adjacent 15th Battalion but, unfortunately, the enemy broke through two platoons. This necessitated the withdrawal of the bulk of the battalion to its reserve line, to the west of Locality C. Only two platoons, those alongside the 2/Buffs, remained in position. As the situation worsened the infantry looked to the artillery for assistance. Such aid that was available was limited, but the 122nd Heavy Battery at Frezenberg took heavy toll of the enemy until late in the afternoon.

The magnitude of the attack on the 13th Battalion gradually increased and before 9.00 a.m. it was forced to retire, towards Locality C. In the confusion the order to retire did not reach the apex. These two gallant units continued to fight until, exhausted and short of ammunition, they were surrounded and either killed or taken prisoner. Lieutenant-General Alderson, at Canadian Divisional headquarters, was informed by Brigadier-General Turner that the 15th Battalion was retiring and that he had ordered the two companies of the 14th and 15th Battalions, in St. Julien, to move forward to counter-attack. In response to this news, Lieutenant-General Alderson ordered two battalions of the 150th (York and Durham) Brigade (Brigadier-General J E Bush) to move from their positions on the canal bank, to points in the GHQ line, to act as reserves to the 2nd and 3rd Infantry Brigades. The 4/East Yorkshire (Lieutenant-Colonel G H Shaw) and the 4/Green Howards (Lieutenant-Colonel M H L Bell) set off for positions adjacent to the two roads from Wieltje, to St. Julien and Fortuin respectively. These two battalions were to be given several sets of conflicting orders before the day was out:

Received orders about midday to concentrate at Wieltje. Crossed the canal under shellfire. We were told we were attached to one of the Canadian brigades. Their brigadier met us and ordered us into the GHQ trenches outside Potijze chateau. He sent a guide with us. On arrival we found the trenches full of troops and being heavily shelled. We lay down behind the trenches while the colonel endeavoured to get orders.

The brigadier of another Canadian brigade ordered us to attack St. Julien. These orders were cancelled and we were told by the 27th Division to dig trenches close to the chateau. Before we fairly started this we were told to attack Fortuin and onto St. Julien. The 4th East Yorks. came with us.[5]

Enfiladed Cross Roads.

In Corps headquarters General Plumer was unsure of the situation. At about 11.30 a.m. he received a message from the 27th Division to the effect that the Canadian line now ran from the left of the 8th Battalion to Locality C and across to St. Julien and Kitchener's Wood. Fearful for the consequences of this breakthrough, he immediately ordered the Canadians to retake the lost ground.

As General Plumer considered his alternatives, the German infantry was again on the move; having stopped to reform after the heavy losses inflicted by the Canadians. The new attack was directed at the Canadian line from Kitchener's Wood to Locality C. At 11.00 a.m. the commanders of the 7th (Major V W Odlum), 14th (Lieutenant-Colonel W W Burland) and 15th (Lieutenant-Colonel J A Currie) Battalions held a hurried meeting at Enfiladed Cross Roads between Locality C and St. Julien. They reluctantly agreed to withdraw to a position covering Fortuin. The new left would be at St. Julien and the right at Locality C. The Canadian withdrawal was executed under extraordinarily heavy artillery fire. During the withdrawal Lieutenant E D Bellew, machine-gun officer of the 7th Canadian Battalion, won the Victoria Cross for conspicuous bravery and devotion to duty **(See chapter 5)**. Some counter-fire was possible, again involving the 122nd Heavy Battery at Frezenberg supported, this time, by several other units. To aid the hard-pressed 3rd Brigade, General Alderson placed the two battalions of the 150th Brigade, moving up to the GHQ Line, at Brigadier-General Turner's disposal. As the attack developed Brigadier-General Turner ordered the two battalions to help with the digging of defences in front of St. Julien. This order proved impossible to fulfil when St. Julien fell to the Germans, and the two battalions were forced to halt at Potijze.

Brigadier-General Turner was already considering the possibility of a more general withdrawal to the GHQ Line, when he received news that reinforcements were on the way from the 27th Division. Lieutenant-General Plumer had made Major-General Snow, commanding that division, responsible for all reserve units. When he became aware of the Canadian 3rd Brigade's withdrawal Major-General Snow sent his own divisional reserve, the 1/Royal Irish, to Fortuin. Before this unit arrived, the three commanders of the 7th, 14th and 15th Battalions met again, this time at the Bombarded Cross Roads where they were joined by Major D M Ormond of the 10th Battalion. In spite of the desire to hold their ground they agreed that a further withdrawal to the Gravenstafel-Wieltje road was inevitable. They were soon proved to be correct, for within fifteen minutes of this meeting the Germans forced the defenders of St. Julien to retire. The right wing of the 3rd Brigade fell back to a line just north of the Gravenstafel-Wieltje road. Brigadier-General Turner felt that withdrawal to the GHQ Line was his only option and at 1.40 p.m. he issued an order to the 3rd Brigade and all attached battalions to hold the GHQ Line from the St. Jean-Poelcappelle road south. This order was issued after two conversations with the divisional G S O 1, Colonel C F Romer. There now existed a gap between Locality C and the left wing of the 2nd Brigade - a gap which contained no troops other than two platoons of the 8th Battalion, north of Boetleer's Farm. Among this small band was Company-Sergeant Major F W Hall, who was to win the Victoria Cross for his efforts to bring in a wounded man **(See chapter 5)**.

The only reserves still available to Major-General Snow were two battalions of the 28th Division: the 1/Suffolk and 12/London (Rangers) which had been relieved by the 2/Cheshire and 1/Monmouthshire during the previous night. Under the impression that Fortuin was in German hands and that there was a gap east of St Julien, he sent orders to Lieutenant-Colonel W B Wallace (Suffolk Regt.) to take the two battalions to Fortuin, accompanied by two companies of the 8/Middlesex as reserve. At about the same time Lieutenant-General Alderson was reinforcing Brigadier-General Turner by bringing forward the Canadian 4th Battalion together with two battalions of the 13th Brigade (5th Division), the 2/KOYLI and the 9/London (Queen Victoria's Rifles). Altogether, there were now five battalions moving towards Fortuin: the two under Lieutenant-Colonel Wallace, the 1/Royal Irish Rifles, the 4/East Yorkshire and the 4/Green Howards. On his way forward Lieutenant-Colonel Wallace was instructed to move to cover the flank of the 2nd Brigade. Unfortunately, in so doing he came under intense artillery fire and suffered heavy casualties and was forced to halt on the Zonnebeke-Keerselare road. From here, two companies of 1/Suffolk were sent to aid the Canadians near Boetleer's Farm, where they were joined by remnants of the 7th and 10th Battalions. In the meantime the 4/East Yorks. and the 4/Green Howards arrived in Fortuin, only to come under fire from the enemy advancing from St. Julien. They immediately changed direction and, together with the 1/Royal Irish Rifles and aided by Canadian artillery, drove the Germans back to the village. In this action Lieutenant-Colonel Shaw was killed, shot through the head. The Germans made no further attempt to advance on the 24th. At night the two battalions of the York and Durham Brigade, now both under the command of Lieutenant-Colonel Bell, together with the Royal Irish Rifles, retired to Potijze. The remaining one and a half battalions of Lieutenant-Colonel Wallace's Detachment withdrew and dug in along the Gravenstafel-Fortuin road.

In the *History of the East Yorkshire Regiment in the Great War*, Everard Wyrall quotes from the report of an unnamed officer who took part in the action and was with Lieutenant-Colonel Shaw when he was killed:

The men behaved as if they were doing an attack practice in peace. It was marvellous. They went on in such a way as if they'd done it all their lives. As soon as it (the attack) developed we were met by high explosive and stinkpots, everybody bobbed, then on again. I accompanied the CO. He and I reached an infernal area when something happened and he never rose again. He was shot through the head by a sniper. I can't express my feelings. Then a hell of a machine-gun fire swept the place. All I could do was to lie 'doggo' – as small as possible. When it was over I went forward and found two platoons of C Company who couldn't advance further. An order then came down to stay where we were till dusk. The enemy's fire ceased and we, after some time, collected up and returned to the trenches. Poor Farrell (Capt. Bede Farrell) was shot through the heart close to me, and Theilman (Major C E Theilman) in the body and he died on the way back.[6]

Captain Bede Farrell.

In an effort to secure the line on the eastern side, the Canadians called upon Major A V Johnson, in command of the 3/Royal Fusiliers, for assistance. This unit was on the extreme left of the British 28th Division and therefore in contact with the Canadian 2nd Brigade. In common with other commanders, Major Johnson had little in the way of reserves at his disposal, except two half companies of the 8/Middlesex. However, in the vicinity of the Bombarded Cross Roads was a working party of the division under Major E M Moulton-Barrett, of the Northumberland Fusiliers. This party, made up of one and a half companies of the 2/Northumberland Fusiliers, two companies of the 2/Cheshire and a company of the 1/Monmouthshire, were moved forward at 8.30 p.m. They joined up with two half companies of the 8/Middlesex and the 1/Suffolk in the vicinity of Boetleer's Farm.

During the afternoon Sir John French communicated his views on the situation in the Salient to Sir Horace Smith-Dorrien. He was adamant that every effort must be made to restore the line about St. Julien in order to protect the 28th Division. However, in a fuller letter, delivered later in the day, he conceded that, if the pressure in the north became too great, the 28th Division could fall back. As already seen the situation on the Canadian front was, to say the least, confused. But was the situation in the French sector any better? Lizerne had fallen during the night, when the German 46th Reserve Division had driven out the French 80th Territorial Brigade. Shortly before this General Foch had issued an order to General Putz, for two major attacks aimed at retaking all the lost ground and driving the enemy back across the canal. The first of these attacks, under General Codet commanding the 306th Brigade, 153rd Division, was to retake Lizerne. The attack was launched at 8.30 a.m. and repeated at 2.00 p.m. It failed to retake Lizerne but did succeed in surrounding the village on three sides. The attack against Het Sas made no progress. In the early afternoon Colonel Mordacq, commanding four battalions of Zouaves, moved out from the canal bank and by nightfall had taken up a continuous line between the canal and the Ypres-Pilckem road.

That the British were fearful for the state of the French, a fear that was to remain for the duration of the battle, was shown by the opening line of a message sent by the Chief of the General Staff, Lieutenant-General Sir William Robertson, to the Second Army at 9.30 a.m. on the 24th:

> *Evidently not much reliance can be placed on the two French
> Divisions on your left.*[7]

Following the failure to retake Lizerne, General Foch assured Sir John French that more divisions were being brought up as quickly as possible - in fact one was already at Cassel and a second would be in the vicinity the following day. On the British side, General Smith-Dorrien placed Lieutenant-General Allenby and his Cavalry Corps at the disposal of General Putz. Lieutenant-General Plumer ordered Lieutenant-General Alderson to counter-attack and, to facilitate this attack, added the 10th and 150th Brigades to his command. At 8 p.m. Lieutenant-General Alderson issued Operation Order No 10:

1. *By orders of the Corps commander a strong counter-attack will be made early tomorrow morning in a general direction of St. Julien with the object of driving the enemy back as far north as possible and thus securing the left flank of the 28th Division.*

2. *Brigadier-General Hull commanding the 10th Brigade will be in charge of this counter-attack.*

3. *The following troops will be placed at the disposal of Brigadier-General Hull for the purpose, viz.:*

4. *10th Infantry Brigade, York & Durham Brigade, 2/KOYLI and Queen Victoria's Rifles of the 13th Brigade, 1st Suffolks and 12th London Regiment of the 28th Division, (Wallace's Detachment) the 4th Canadian Battalion and one battalion of the 27th Division (1/Royal Irish Rifles). The first objectives will be Fortuin (if occupied by the enemy), St. Julien and the wood in C.10 and C.11 (Kitchener's Wood).*[8]

This was a considerable force, consisting as it did of fifteen battalions, although in the event only five would take part. The attack was set for 3.30 a.m. next day, 25 April.

On another part of the battlefield a German, Rudolph Binding, was recording his thoughts on the second gas attack in his diary:

The effects of the successful gas attack were horrible. I am not pleased with the idea of poisoning men. Of course, the entire world will rage about it first and then imitate us. All the dead lie on their backs, with clenched fists; the whole field is yellow. They say that Ypres must fall now. One can see it burning – not without a pang for the beautiful city. Langemarck is a heap of rubbish, and all rubbish heaps look alike; there is no sense in describing one. All that remains of the church is the doorway with the date 1620.[9]

The 3.30 a.m. attack was doomed to failure from the outset. No time was available for reconnaissance or for getting the battalions into position. Such a large attack would have been difficult to organise in daylight: but at night, under fire and in heavy rain, over unknown ground, it was impossible! Although Lieutenant-General Alderson's order had contained a reference point to which the battalion commanders were to report, only two did so. It was left to Brigadier-General Hull to set up his headquarters at Mouse Trap Farm and then to set out himself to find his command. Nor was his intelligence up to date, for at midnight, both St. Julien and Fortuin were unoccupied. Once established at Mouse Trap Farm Brigadier-General Hull postponed the attack until 5.30 a.m., a delay which was not communicated to the supporting artillery. By the time the attack took place the preliminary bombardment had long ceased.

When the units of the 10th Brigade arrived at the GHQ Line they discovered that there were only two breaks in the wire through which they could move out. Unable to communicate with the other elements of his command, Brigadier-General Hull ordered the four regular battalions of the Brigade to deploy in the front line westwards from Fortuin. The remaining Territorial battalion was to remain in support behind the left flank. The 1/Royal Irish Fusiliers and 2/Royal Dublin Fusiliers were positioned on the right and left of the Haanebeek at Fortuin and directed on St. Julien. The 1/Royal Warwickshire Regiment, with the 7/Argyll and Sutherland Highlanders supporting, were to attack Kitchener's Wood. The 2/Seaforth Highlanders were to move on the German trenches between the wood and St. Julien, connecting the left and right attacks.

The five battalions made their way through the wire and moved to the start positions and as day broke they moved forward. Soon, however, heavy rifle and machine-gun fire, from St. Julien and the adjacent buildings, began to cut swathes through the lines. Since midnight the German 51st Reserve Division had moved forward and was in the process of reoccupying St. Julien. The 1/Royal Irish Fusiliers were stopped two hundred yards from the village, while the 1/Royal Dublin Fusiliers, after over-running Vanheule Farm, were also stopped short of the outskirts. The 2/Seaforth Highlanders, although reinforced by the 7/Argyll and Sutherland Highlanders at 6 a.m., were stopped five hundred yards from Kitchener's Wood. The 1/Royal Warwickshire were also stopped well short of their objective. Eventually a new line was established with its apex at Vanheule Farm, five hundred yards from the edge of St. Julien. They were to remain in these positions for several days. The brigade suffered very heavy casualties, over seventy officers and in excess of two thousand other ranks. Its fighting strength was reduced by fifty percent.

Before and after the abortive attack other units of Hull's force moved into position or were made aware of the new situation. On the right, Lieutenant-Colonel Wallace ordered the two battalions, which were now under Brigadier-General Hull's command, to remain where they were. The Canadian 1st and 4th Battalions moved forward of Wieltje, where they remained in support. The 5/Green Howards and the 5/Durham Light Infantry, two battalions of the York and Durham Brigade, were sent orders to move to their right through Fortuin. Due to a misunderstanding they did not take up position until late morning. While awaiting the arrival of these two battalions Brigadier-General

Hull ordered two battalions of the 149th Brigade, the 4/Northumberland and the 7/Northumberland Fusiliers, to positions south of Fortuin. This brigade had been added to his force from corps reserve. The 2/KOYLI, the Queen Victoria's Rifles and the 1/Royal Irish Rifles were detailed to the reserve.

The German plans changed, significantly, on 25 April. The Army Commander, General Duke Albrecht von Württemberg, ordered that the actions against the French should be halted, but that the ground already gained must be consolidated and held. At the same time the XXVI Reserve Corps should renew attacks in its sector, with the object of cutting off the British and Canadian forces in the Salient. In accordance with this order two unsuccessful attacks were launched during the day. The first, at 5 a.m., fell on the 28th Division and the second, at 3.30 p.m., on the front of the 2nd Canadian Brigade in the vicinity of Boetleer's Farm.

In the course of the day the 11th Brigade (Brigadier-General J Hasler) and the Lahore Division (Major-General H D'U Keary) arrived in the vicinity of Ypres. With these additional resources Lieutenant-General Plumer decided to reorganise his Corps front. He made Major-General Bulfin additionally responsible for the sectors held by the Canadian 2nd Brigade and by units on the Canadian left up to the Fortuin-St. Julien road. Lieutenant-General Alderson's command was consequently restricted to the line from the same road to the junction with the French. Within each command he ordered the generals to get as many troops as possible back under their proper commanders. At about the same time as this order was produced, Brigadier-General Currie ordered the 2nd Canadian to retire southwards as a

Brigadier-General J Hasler.

result of the German assault. This retirement necessitated a similar realignment by the 3/Royal Fusiliers, who moved into part of Berlin Wood. There followed a night of intense activity as units moved to their new positions.

> *On receipt of General Plumer's 2.30 p.m. orders to reorganise his line, General Alderson directed Brigadier-General Hull to hold his front from Fortuin to Mouse Trap Farm with his own brigade and the 1/Royal Irish Fusiliers; Brigadier-General Wanless O'Gowan to take over the front of Geddes's Detachment from Mouse Trap Farm to the French with the 13th Brigade, then in reserve west of the canal, the 2/KOYLI and the Queen Victoria's Rifles having rejoined it, and the 4/Rifle Brigade of the*

27th Division being attached. Geddes's four battalions in the front line were to go back to Potijze, but his reserve of three battalions was to remain at St. Jean. The 149th Brigade was ordered to the south of Wieltje, as General Alderson's reserve. The 1st Canadian Brigade was sent back across the canal.[10]

Brigadier-General Hasler was instructed by General Bulfin to move his brigade to the right and to take over command of the Canadian 2nd Brigade, together with all the detachments in the sector between the 85th Brigade and St. Julien-Fortuin road. In an effort to produce a solid defensive line across his designated sector, before dawn Brigadier-General Hasler dispatched one battalion, the 1/Hampshire (Lieutenant-Colonel F R Hicks), to join up with the 85th Brigade while the remainder of the 11th Brigade moved towards Fortuin from St. Jean. The 1/Hampshire linked up with the left of the 3/Royal Fusiliers, replacing the Canadian 5th and 8th Battalions, and by early morning had dug themselves in on a line close to Gravenstafel village. The remainder of the brigade eventually ended up on the Zonnebeke ridge in the vicinity of Point 37 **(See map 1 page 17)**. The line achieved was by no means solid, there were several large gaps, but it had been improved. Later, some of the exposed units withdrew to a line along the Zonnebeke ridge.

There remained the question - how best to utilise the Lahore Division? The French had still not carried out their promised attack - the reinforcements were still awaited. However, in concert with the British, General Putz had also reorganised his force. In order to attack on the 26th he created two wings under General Quiquandon and General Deligny. His plan was for an attack by seventeen battalions at 5.00 p.m., later revised to 2.00 p.m. In spite of the short time available and the necessity of an all night march for the Indian Division, at Sir John French's insistence, General Smith–Dorrien agreed to co-operate.

Second Army Operation Order No. 8 was issued at 2.15 a.m. on 26 April.[11] It stated that the French were to carry out an attack, on their front with their right on the Ypres-Langemarck road. It then detailed the roles to be played by the Lahore Division and troops under General Alderson's command, in an elaborate plan to recapture much of the recently lost ground. The Lahore Division was ordered to march via Ypres to a position north of an area Wieltje-St. Jean and to deploy with its left on the Ypres-Langemarck road. It was then to advance, through V Corps positions to attack in the direction of Langemarck, on a thousand-yard front.

The order also listed artillery support requirements and directed V Corps to co-operate in the attack. General Alderson, on receipt of this order, via General Plumer, issued his own Operation Order, No. 12, at 12.15 p.m. He instructed a battalion of the 10th Brigade to advance with the Lahore Division, between Kitchener's Wood and the Wieltje-St. Julien road, and at the same time the 149th (Northumbrian) Brigade (Brigadier-General J F Riddell) to attack astride the same road.

The three infantry brigades of the Lahore Division each consisted of one British Regular, one British Territorial and three Indian battalions. The Division moved to its positions of assembly as follows:

The Ferozepore Brigade started at 5.30 a.m. and proceeded to St. Jean via Vlamertinghe.

The Jullundur Brigade, ordered to Wieltje, set out at 7.30 a.m. and passed to the south of Ypres.

The Sirhind Brigade, detailed as divisional reserve, followed the route taken by the Ferozepore Brigade, to a position south-east of St. Jean.

The Jullundur Brigade (Brigadier-General E P Strickland), while passing close to the ramparts of Ypres, came under heavy shellfire. Unfortunately, one large shell fell into the middle of the 40th Pathans, causing twenty-two casualties. As the Brigade formed up in the fields near Wieltje, still under constant fire, more shells fell among the 1/Manchester, causing further casualties. The Ferozepore Brigade (Brigadier-General R G Egerton) and the Sirhind Brigade (Brigadier-

General Egerton commanding the Ferozepore Brigade, in the streets of Wytschaete, October 1914. IWM Q 56320

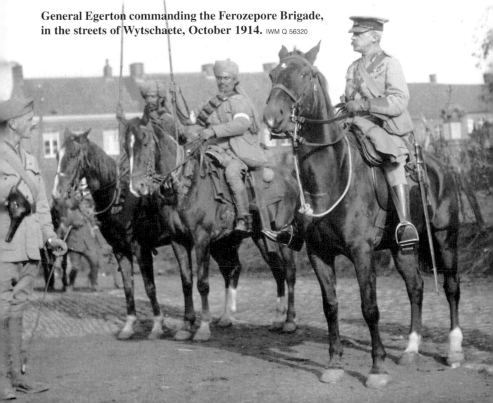

Brigadier-General J F Riddell.

General W G Walker) also came under fire on their way to St. Jean. The three brigades were in position by 11.00 a.m., but it was not until 12.30 that they left for their positions of deployment.

The other two components of Lieutenant-General Alderson's force received their orders almost too late to act upon them. Brigadier-General Riddell's instructions to move forward did not reach him until 1.10 p.m., only ten minutes before they were supposed to start. He set out at 1.50 p.m. only to discover that, to reach the start line, he had to pass through the defences of the GHQ Line. Similarly, Brigadier-General Hull received his orders at 1.25 p.m. He spoke by telephone with Lieutenant-General Alderson explaining that it was not possible for him to get a battalion into position at the time stated. However, he went forward to the line held by the 7/Argyll and Sutherland Highlanders and alerted their commanding officer. He ordered him to attack when he saw action in the vicinity of Kitchener's Wood.

While these preparations were going forward the Germans were not entirely idle. Their artillery, guided by excellent fields of view, was punishing any signs of movement. Further attacks on the XXVI Reserve Corps front had been delayed, for several days, to permit completion of the installation of gas cylinders. The programme had already been in progress for several days so that some cylinders were already in position on the 52nd Reserve Division front, a fact that was to bear greatly upon the French attack. However, on the right of the British line, from early morning and during the remainder of the day, fierce fighting took place. The enemy made repeated attempts to create a gap between Berlin Wood and the cross roads to the south-west of Gravenstafel. In the course of the day the line was pushed back behind Boetleer's Farm, a reverse which had the effect of removing a Salient from the British line.

For the French attack, as has already been noted, General Putz had created two wings. The right wing, adjacent to the British, was further subdivided. General Joppé, commanding his own 152nd Division and troops under Colonel Mordacq, was to attack in the direction of Pilckem. To his left and on the other bank of the canal, troops directly under General Quiquandon would stand ready to move through Boesinghe if General Joppé's attack succeeded.

Joppé's group made an advance of about 150 metres during the afternoon in the centre and on the right. At noon the 4th Moroccan

72

*Brigade (152nd Division) began to cross the canal further south
and beyond Mordacq's Detachment, to take up a position on the
right of Joppé's right. At 2.00 p.m. it attacked in conjunction with
the Lahore Division, which had just reinforced the English left,
upon the axis: Ypres-Langemarck road. The advance was
unexpectedly stopped by a discharge of gas and the troops driven
back in some places to the south of their jumping-off places.
Morteldje Farm was evacuated and then recaptured at 6.00 p.m.* [12]

The limited progress made by Joppé's group did not allow of any
attempt by Quiquandon's group to cross the canal at Boesinghe.

The Jullundur Brigade, its right resting on Wieltje Farm, occupied a
front of some five hundred yards. The Ferozepore Brigade continued
the line to the left as far as the Ypres-Langemarck road, where touch
was gained with the French **(See map 13 page 77)**. From right to left
the units in the front line were 1/Manchester, 40th Pathans, 47th Sikhs
(Jullundur Brigade), 129th Baluchis, 57th Rifles and the Connaught
Rangers (Ferozepore Brigade). The total length of front was about one
thousand yards and the average distance to the enemy line just over a
mile. Behind the front line, at a distance of some two hundred and fifty
yards, each brigade had support. The 59th Rifles and the 4/Suffolk
were on the right and the 4/London on the left. The 9th Bhopal Infantry
was in reserve with orders to move, in the first instance, to the trenches
occupied by the Rangers.

Indian cavalry in northern France 1915. TAYLOR LIBRARY

Turco Farm and Mauser ridge from Boundary Road.

The French assault was timed for 2.00 p.m., and that for the Lahore Division, echeloned slightly in the rear of the French, was set five minutes earlier. The ground over which the attack was to be made was perfectly open and devoid of cover. For the first five or six hundred yards it rose slightly, then there was a decline for about another six hundred yards before it rose again to the line of the German front trench. From the top of the first crest the enemy's front line could be seen clearly. The general direction of the attack was due north. When the bombardment commenced, at 1.20 p.m., the attacking troops advanced intending to get as far forward as possible before the barrage lifted to a line two hundred yards beyond the enemy front. Unfortunately, the Jullundur Brigade under machine-gun fire from small farms north-east of Canadian Farm, moved in a direction to the west of north. This resulted in it crowding in on the Ferozepore Brigade, forcing it to overlap the road which formed the dividing line between the Indian and French Divisions. In the ensuing confusion portions of all the leading battalions became intermingled.

On the extreme right the 1/Manchester made good progress, in spite of the enemy's intense fire, until they crossed the ridge. Here they began to be cut to pieces. Within seconds only one officer, Second Lieutenant Williamson-Jones, was standing and he too was soon hit. Corporal Issy Smith **(See chapter 5)** was awarded the Victoria Cross for his bravery in helping the wounded. Eventually the leading troops reached a road only sixty yards in front of the enemy line. As the afternoon wore on the casualties mounted, culminating at 9.30 p.m. in the death of the commanding officer, Lieutenant-Colonel H W E Hitchens; he was struck by a bullet while crossing the ground between the British and French trenches. In total the battalion sustained nearly three hundred casualties.

The leading companies of the 40th Pathans, the unit to the left of the 1/Manchester, also made good ground until they reached the ridge; where they too began to fall. Less fortunate were the units in the rear, which suffered heavily as by then the German machine-gunners had the ground fully swept. Only three hundred yards from the assault trench the commanding officer, Lieutenant-Colonel F R Rennick, fell mortally wounded. The Battalion Adjutant, Lieutenant Campbell, managed to drag him into a ditch, where he lay until dusk. At that time he was brought in and accompanied by two of his Pathans was placed in a motor ambulance. He died later that night, on the journey to Hazebrouck, where he was buried in the communal cemetery.

The battalion machine-guns were carried forward at the rear of the attack. On reaching the crest they found that they could not bring their guns to bear, so the officer in charge, Lieutenant Munn, ordered a few men to accompany him forward to a better position. These leading troops set off with the ammunition, while the rest followed with the guns. At the bottom of the slope he found a good position near a beek but the men carrying the guns were cut down before they could join their comrades. Sepoy Muktiara at once volunteered to bring up one of the guns, and succeeded in crossing the two hundred and fifty yards of open ground. Unfortunately, the gun had been damaged and when set up would not operate. It was later recovered and brought back. For his gallantry Lieutenant Munn was awarded the Military Cross.

Still intent on reaching the enemy lines the 40th Pathans pressed on in short rushes, but their losses increased. Captain J F C Dalmahoy led his men to a point within 50 yards of the enemy lines before being hit for the fifth time and killed. Major A C Perkins was also hit just short of his objective and died of his wounds two days later. In their attempts to get at the Germans the 40th Pathans lost over three hundred officers and men.

The 47th Sikhs fared even worse. Although heavily shelled they managed to get into their allocated position on the brigade extreme left, but as the attack developed the loss of direction, mentioned above, led to confusion. Casualties rose rapidly as they moved forward and by the end of the action their numbers had been reduced by over a quarter.

Ground on which Lahore Brigade formed up on 26 April 1915, from Buff's Road.

50TH DIVISION MEMORIAL

The toll was particularly heavy among the officers whose numbers, at roll call next day, had fallen from twenty-one to four.

The attack by the Ferozepore Brigade mirrored that of the Jullundur Brigade. On the right the 129th Baluchis tried to move forward in spite of the cramping effect of the general movement off line. When they reached the crest many men either fell or sought cover in the remnants of farm buildings. Inspired by their officers to renew their efforts they eventually reached a point within three hundred yards of the Germans but were then stopped. The centre battalion, the 57th Rifles, were fortunate in the early stages, suffering few casualties, but once the ridge was reached they too lost heavily. The remnants managed to get within eighty yards of the enemy line before being stopped. On the extreme left the Connaught Rangers, having already had losses in reaching their position of deployment, found that their path was hampered by a series of hedges. As they tried to move out under cover of the bombardment they lost time negotiating these obstacles, with the result that they felt the full effects of the enemy's fire. In common with all the other units, the majority of their casualties occurred on the ridge. The casualty returns for the action show losses in excess of thirty percent of the initial strength.

The front line battalions of both brigades were now in advanced positions, unable to move and with very little available cover. However, bad as the position appeared, it soon became much worse; the chlorine gas, which halted the French, reached the Lahore Division. Lacking any means of protection, the troops of the Ferozepore Brigade and to a lesser extent those of the Jullundur Brigade were soon suffering the terrible agony of gas. Forced to fall back, they suffered further heavy casualties from enhanced German fire. In the ensuing chaos Jemadar Mir Dast, 55th Coke's Rifles attached to the 57th Rifles, helped steady the line and brought several British and Indian officers to safety. He was subsequently awarded the Victoria Cross **(See chapter 5)**.

The attack by the Lahore Division got nowhere near Kitchener's Wood, so that the 7/Argyll and Sutherland Highlanders took no part in the action. On the other hand the three battalions of the 149th (Northumberland) Brigade* were to suffer casualties in excess of those of the Lahore Division.

It was 2.5 p.m. before the leading battalion reached the GHQ Line. No sooner had they deployed on both sides of the Wieltje-St. Julien road than they came under very heavy shell and rifle fire. The thick wire entanglements in front of the GHQ Line, not having been reconnoitred, caused delay and heavy losses, for the

* The 5/Northumberland Fusiliers did not take part.

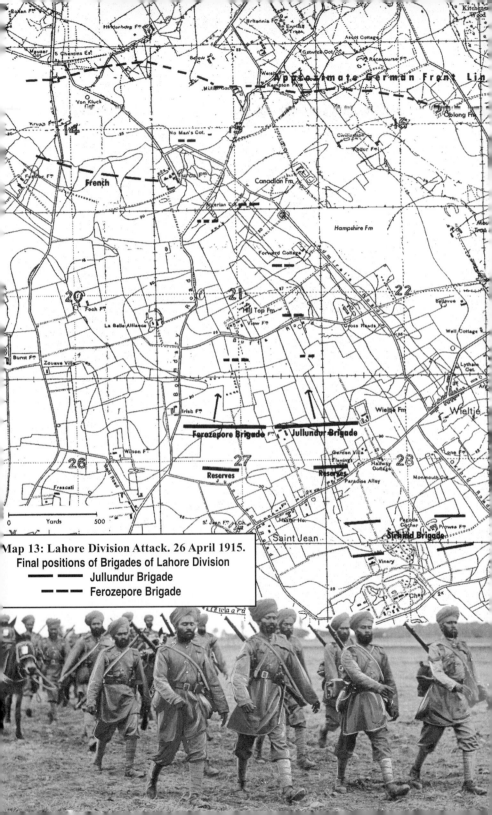

Map 13: Lahore Division Attack. 26 April 1915.
Final positions of Brigades of Lahore Division

——— Jullundur Brigade
– – – Ferozepore Brigade

men were bound to bunch together in order to get through the gaps.

By 2.45 p.m. the 4th and 6th Battalions had reached the front line where they were to find the battalion of the 10th Brigade, which was to connect the Northumberland Brigade with the Lahore Division on the left. By now the 7th Battalion had been absorbed into the line. No troops of the 10th Brigade were seen.

But, pushing on with the greatest dash without artillery support, isolated parties of the 6th Battalion reached positions about two hundred and fifty yards in front of the front trench and occupied some small trenches from which the enemy had apparently retired. The 4th and 7th Battalions were unable to get beyond the front line mentioned.[13]

At 3.45 p.m. the Brigade lost its commanding officer. At that time Brigadier-General Riddell went forward, accompanied by his Brigade Major, to confer with his battalion commanders. At a point about one hundred and fifty yards south of Vanheule Farm he was hit in the head and died instantly. He had had the honour of leading the first Territorial Brigade (as such) to go into battle in the war. He is buried in Tyne Cot Cemetery. Command of the Brigade passed to Colonel Foster of the 4th Battalion, who ordered the three battalions to dig in as best they could. They remained in these positions until withdrawn, to Wieltje, early the following day. In this attack the Brigade lost over forty officers and two thousand other ranks.

During the night of 26/27 April the Sirhind Brigade relieved the Jullundur and Ferozepore Brigades. With the help of the 3rd Sappers and Miners and a company of the 34th Sikh Pioneers, they proceeded to consolidate the front line. The Jullundur and Ferozepore Brigades withdrew to La Brique. Also during the night reconnaissance parties were sent into No Man's Land to ascertain more details of the enemy's positions. Carried out under the almost continuous release of flares and the fire of rifle and machine-guns, the information gained permitted more definite plans to be laid for any future attacks.

By the evening of 26 April the situation in the Salient was becoming more and more difficult for the British. The only gain during the day was made during the afternoon, when a joint Franco-Belgian operation recovered most of the village of Lizerne. The German guns controlled the whole area: any movement of men or supplies always brought down a storm of steel. The opportunity for retaliation was limited by lack of heavy artillery pieces and by shortages of munitions, but the Second Army could look for little help. An attack by General Haig's First Army

Map 14: Lahore Division Attack. 27 April 1915.
Starting positions of Brigades of Lahore Division
— — Jullundur Brigade
— — Ferozepore Brigade
— — — Sirhind Brigade

0   Yards   500

was imminent and General Smith-Dorrien knew that Sir John French would be loath to hazard that undertaking by transferring any supplies or men to the Ypres area.

During the night of the 26/27 April General Putz issued orders for the offensive to be resumed the next day. The objectives were identical to those of the previous day, but the orders included some changes in the units to take part. He once more asked for the British to co-operate, on his right, the boundary between the forces again being the Ypres-Langemarck road. A preliminary bombardment lasting forty-five minutes was to precede the attack, which was scheduled for 1.15 p.m. General Smith-Dorrien agreed that the Lahore Division would co-operate but with the proviso that they would not be employed until the French had made significant progress thus, securing the British left flank. For some unknown reason the Lahore Division ignored this caveat.

The scheme required that, following a bombardment timed to start at 12.30 p.m. the French Moroccan troops on the right of the Ypres-Langemarck road would attack at 1.30 p.m. **(See map 14 page 79)**. Under the cover of the bombardment the Ferozepore Brigade would move back into the line and come up alongside the Sirhind Brigade. However, as soon as the bombardment started the Ferozepore Brigade began to move forward but the Sirhind Brigade commander, Brigadier-General W G Walker, did not wait for it to arrive, instead he too advanced at the start of the bombardment. The Brigade advanced on a two battalion front, the 1/4th Gurkhas (Major B M L Brodhurst) on the right and the 1/1st Gurkhas (Lieutenant-Colonel W C Anderson) on the left. In passing the ridge the attack came under severe cross-fire from rifles and machine-guns as well as from several other directions. Major Brodhurst was killed early in the attack, but three officers and about thirty men of the 1/4th managed to reach Canada Farm. In this isolated position they held on until late afternoon when, in a splendid action, led by their commanding officer Lieutenant-Colonel J W Allen, a party of the 4th King's reinforced them.

The 1/1st Gurkhas, like the 1/4th, suffered severely from heavy enfilade fire on their way to some enclosed ground on the downward slope, being compelled to swing round towards the left to face it. Some few men got to within two hundred yards of the enemy line but the bulk of the battalion was held at a distance of four hundred yards. Although the objective was not reached, the 1/1st established a position in advance of some French guns, which had been abandoned, and during the night these were safely removed. In the meantime the Ferozepore Brigade, led by the 4/London and 9th Bhopals, had been moving forward, but they fell into a devastating fire from artillery, rifles and machine-guns, which almost stopped them in their tracks.

Admiral's Road. The building on the left is Canadian Farm. The original farm was behind this building.

However, a few managed to link up with the Sirhind troops near Canadian Farm.

The Second Army had foreseen the need to have reinforcements available to the Lahore Division. Consequently, a composite unit was made up and put under the command of Lieutenant-Colonel H D Tuson (Duke of Cornwall's Light Infantry). Although designated to be of brigade strength, in reality it was nearer that of a battalion, consisting as it did of just 1,290 men drawn from four regiments: 2/D.C.L.I., 1/York and Lancaster, 5/King's Own and 2/Duke of Wellington's. Following a further bombardment the attack was to be renewed, on both fronts. But the French attacked before the British were ready and again failed to make progress. When the two Lahore Brigades and Tuson's Detachment eventually attacked, at 6.30 p.m., they were similarly cut down. What little ground they gained had to be given up when the French troops on their left withdrew under heavy gas shelling. By nightfall the lines of the morning had been re-established.

The only significant gain made on the 27th was that by General Codet, who completed the seizure of Lizerne but failed to reach Steenstraat.

While these actions had been taking place at the front, important events were occurring behind the lines. On receipt of General Putz's orders for the operations on the 27th, General Smith-Dorrien was so 'horrified' that he set down his thoughts in a long letter to Lieutenant-General Sir William Robertson, Chief of the General Staff at British G.H.Q. This letter is of such significance that its text is reproduced, in full, in appendix five

In essence he was expressing a lack of confidence in the French and his expectation that no progress would be made that day, which proved to be the case. He also laid out, in detail, his thoughts on the condition of the troops in the Salient and how best they might be improved, by a tactical withdrawal. He made it quite clear that, although he was not being pessimistic, he felt he must be prepared to deal with the situation that could arise if the enemy made further progress. In any case, the withdrawal he proposed was one that could not be carried out easily, given the size of the problem. However, in the absence of any major events, he intended to withdraw some troops to a safer line, west of Ypres.

Sir John French reacted swiftly to this letter. At 2.15 p.m. Sir William Robertson telephoned General Smith-Dorrien with Sir John's reply:

> *Chief does not regard situation nearly so unfavourable as your letter represents. He thinks you have abundance of troops and especially notes the large reserves you have. He wishes you to act vigorously with the full means available in co-operating with and assisting the French having regard to his previous instructions that the combined attack should be simultaneous. The French possession of Lizerne and general situation on the canal seems to remove anxiety as to your left flank. Letter follows by Staff Officer.*[14]

The staff officer was Major-General E M Perceval, Sub-Chief of the General Staff, who arrived at General Smith-Dorrien's headquarters shortly after Sir William Robertson's telephone call. In a letter to the British Official Historian, in 1936, Major-General Perceval confirmed that he had taken a message to General Smith-Dorrien and quoted Smith-Dorrien's comment:

> *'As you know, whatever I do will be wrong'* meaning that French would find fault with him in any case.[15]

That General Smith-Dorrien was correct in this assumption did not take long to emerge. At 4.35 p.m. a telegram arrived at Second Army headquarters from Sir John French. Somewhat unusually the telegram was despatched 'in clear' and so was readable by all who saw it:

Brigadier-General E M Perceval.

> *Chief directs you to hand over forthwith to General Plumer the command of all troops engaged in the*

present operations about Ypres. You should lend General Plumer
your Brigadier-General General Staff and such other officers of
the various branches of your staff as he may require. General
Plumer should send all reports direct to G.H.Q. from which he
will receive his orders. Acknowledge.

  Addressed to Second Army repeated V Corps.[16]

The actual transfer of responsibility took place at 5.30 p.m. At 8.00
p.m. 'Plumer's Force' came into existence.

That night, on another part of the battlefield, Rudolph Biding was
again writing in his diary:

Last night I salved three captured guns that were lying in full
view of the enemy's new line, not more than five hundred metres
away. The moon was shining, and apart from this, the enemy kept
the battlefield continually lighted up with most damnable bright
Very lights. We were all night on the job, constantly interrupted
by furious bursts of fire and by the Very lights, which obliged us
to lie flat on the ground as long as they were burning. Before
dawn we got all three guns into safety, together with their
limbers and ammunition. One of my men was shot through the
heart because he tried to bring back a sucking pig, which he
found squeaking in its lonely pen on one of the limbers. He sat
on top, while his comrades put their shoulders to the wheels.
Suddenly he fell lifeless between the wheels, still holding his little
pig in the grip of death.

After fresh attacks a sleeping army lies in front of one of our
brigades; they rest in good order, man by man, and will never
wake again – Canadian divisions. The enemy's losses are
enormous.

The battlefield is fearful. One is overcome by a peculiar sour,
heavy, and penetrating smell of corpses. Rising over a plank
bridge you find that its middle is supported only by the body of
a long-dead horse. Men that were killed last October lie half in
a swamp and half in the yellow-sprouting beet-fields, the legs of

*an Englishman, still encased in puttees, stick out into a trench,
the corpse being built into the parapet; a soldier hangs his rifle
on them. A little brook runs through the trench and everyone uses
the water for drinking and washing; it is the only water we have.
Nobody minds the pale Englishman who is rotting away a few
steps further up. In Langemarck cemetery a hecatomb had been
piled up; for the dead must have lain above ground-level.
German shells falling into it started a horrible resurrection. At
one point I saw twenty-two dead horses, still harnessed,
accompanied by a few dead drivers. Cattle and pigs lie about,
half-rotten; broken trees, avenues razed to the ground; crater
upon crater in the roads and in the fields. Such is a six months
old battlefield.*[17]

Bibliography

1. *Official History of the Canadian Forces in the Great War 1914-1919*. Volume I. Col. A. F. Duguid. Ottawa 1938.
2. Public Record Office. CAB 45/156.
3. *War Diary Canadian 10th Battalion*. Public Record Office. WO 95/3370.
4. *The History of the 16th Battalion in the Great War*. Macmillan. Toronto. 1932.
5. *War Diary 4/Yorkshire Regiment (Green Howards)*. Public Record Office. WO 95/2836.
6. *The East Yorkshire Regiment in the Great War*. Everard Wyrall. Harrison & Sons. London. 1928.
7. Public Record Office. CAB 45/206.
8. *War Diary 1st Canadian Division*. Public Record Office. WO 95/3717.
9. *A Fatalist at War*. Rudolph Binding. Houghton Mifflin Company. 1929.
10. *Military Operations in France & Belgium*. 1915 Volume 1. Edmonds. Macmillan 1927.
11. *War Diary Second Army. General Staff*. Public Record Office. WO 95/270.
12. *Les Armées Françaises dans la Grande Guerre*. Tome II. Part 3.
13. *The History of the 50th Division 1914 – 1919*. E. Wyrall. Percy Lund, Humphries & Co. London 1939.
14. *Military Operations in France & Belgium*. 1915 Volume 1. Edmonds. Macmillan 1927.
15. Public Record Office. CAB 45/206.
16. *Ibid*.
17. *A Fatalist at War*. Rudolph Binding. Houghton Mifflin Company. 1929.

Chapter Four

REORGANISATION AND WITHDRAWAL

With the creation of 'Plumer's Force', Lieutenant-General Plumer became not only General Officer Commanding the new force, but remained in the same post for V Corps: the only difference was that he now reported directly to G.H.Q. instead of through Second Army. With irony, which was probably lost on the Commander-in-Chief, the first orders he received in the new role directed him to do almost exactly what Sir Horace Smith-Dorrien had suggested.

The Chief wishes you to consolidate the line you now hold so as to render it more secure against attack.

You are also requested to prepare a line east of Ypres joining up with the line now held north and south of that place ready for

Germans in St Julien in 1915.

occupation if and when it becomes advisable to withdraw from the present salient. Please report early as to the position of the line you select for this purpose. It should be such as to avoid withdrawal from Hill 60. The necessary instructions, if any, will be sent by G.H.Q. to Second Corps on receipt of your report.[1]

General Plumer immediately set about reorganising his new command. Colonel Geddes' battalions were returned to their own brigades, as were all troops belonging to the 27th and 28th Divisions. In addition the latter division was also given the 11th, 150th and 151st Brigades. Three brigades, the 10th, 13th and 149th were sent to Lieutenant-General Alderson. These changes were carried out during the night of the 27/28 April. The enemy did not interfere directly but continued to shell the whole area. All roads, crossings and villages, or what remained of them, were systematically targeted. Early on the 28 April Sir John French met with General Foch at Cassel, to apprise him of his concerns for the situation in the British sector. He intimated his intention to withdraw, an action, which was vigorously opposed by General Foch. Sir John finally acquiesced to General Foch's pleadings

Map 15: Plumer's new line. 3 May 1915.

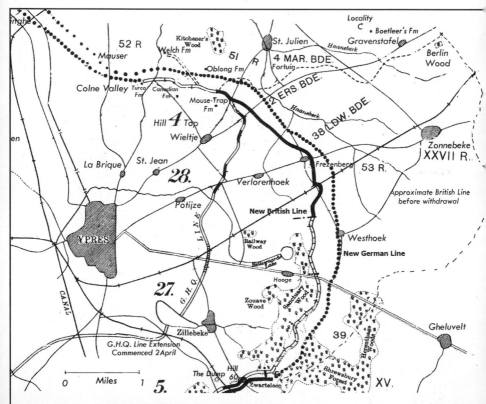

that he at least delay any such action until after the next French attack, planned for later in the afternoon. However, the British Commander-in Chief again contacted Lieutenant-General Plumer and repeated his instruction to prepare for withdrawal.

The French attacks on the 28 April, even in the words of the official French historian, 'brought but light results'. The enemy was overpowered in wooded area between Het Sas and Lizerne but the attackers were stopped in front of Steenstraat. As before, lack of success prevented General Quiquandon from crossing the canal. According to the French, the enemy again employed poison gas in repelling the attacks, but the German accounts state that the French were driven back by gun fire alone.

Even as these attacks were in progress Lieutenant-General Plumer was preparing his plans for the new line. In a document, sent to G.H.Q., on the afternoon of 28 April, he detailed his proposals. The new line would run northwards from Hill 60, cross the Menin road in front of Hooge, and then through Westhoek to the Frezenberg ridge. From there it would swing to the left, towards Mouse Trap Farm, before running westwards to the canal **(See map 15 page 86)**. By adopting this scheme he considered that a defensible line would be established. He added that he considered that the withdrawal would be essential unless the French regained all their lost ground, and would require at least four nights for completion.

At a further meeting between the French and British commanders, on the morning of 29 April, agreement was reached on a joint attack for the following day, an attack which, if not successful, would be followed by the British withdrawal. The scheme involved: an attack by General Curé's group on ground near Steenstraat with a view to reaching the canal bank, while General Quiquandon's group would be prepared to debauch through Boesinghe in concert with the left of General Joppé's group. The main thrust was to be made by General Joppé's group against the German line between the canal and the Ypres-Langemarck road, with Pilckem as the final objective. In preparation for the attack the French had made an independent attack on Steenstraat village at 6.00 p.m. on the 29th and managed to enter the village but failed to drive the enemy off the west bank of the canal. The British unit involved was to be the Sirhind Brigade, which was ordered to advance with the French, to protect their right flank, and to maintain connection between the two armies. The attack was set for 8.00 a.m. but due to thick fog was postponed until 11.15 a.m. Although General Joppé's left made some slight progress his right, adjacent to the British, did not advance. Consequently, the Sirhind Brigade remained in their trenches behind Hill Top ridge. Once again General Quiquandon was prevented from moving by the failure of supporting actions. Later in the day the French requested British support for another, more limited attack, the next day. As this proposal also involved a change in direction, Lieutenant-General Plumer agreed to provide artillery support but no troops, unless as part of a general French offensive east of the canal. During the evening General Foch visited Sir John French at his headquarters at Hazebrouck. Reluctantly, Sir John French agreed to a further twenty-four hour postponement of the withdrawal, to give General Putz more time. During the night one British relief was carried out, the 12th Brigade (4th Division) took over the left sector of the front of the 10th Brigade and the whole of that of the 13th Brigade.

On 1 May General Putz's plan was to exploit the meagre results of the previous day. He regrouped the 45th Division under the orders of General Quiquandon. General Joppé who only commanded the 4th Moroccan Brigade and the 35th Brigade, was reinforced with one regiment from the Army Reserve. The common objective of the two groups was to be Pilckem, the eastern part of which General Joppé would attack while making an effort to occupy the area between the village and the Ypres-Langemarck road. General Quiquandon's right (General Mordacq) would take possession of the ridge west of Pilckem. General Curé would continue at his task of clearing the

The village of St Julien when under German occupation.

enemy from the left bank of the canal. The attacks were all to go in at 3.10 p.m. The Sirhind Brigade was again given the task of co-operating with the French, but again only if the attack won ground.

At 3.10 p.m. under the cover of artillery fire the attack was launched - or more correctly the attack was supposed to be launched – for the French infantry did not leave their trenches. A second attempt, timed for 4.40 p.m., also failed to materialise. In truth the men were just too tired to make any further effort. But the failures may well have saved expenditure of lives unnecessarily. General Foch had been informed, by General Joffre that the operations in the Arras–Neuve Chapelle theatre were to take precedence and that accordingly Foch was to adopt a defensive stance around Ypres. Consequently, when the first failure of the afternoon's actions became known, the order was issued to Lieutenant-General Plumer to commence the planned withdrawal that same night.

The first unit to be brought back was the Lahore Division, which was relocated to Ouderdom, about 5 miles from Ypres. At the same time artillery belonging to the Canadian Division and the British 27th Division was moved back to Brielen and closer to the canal respectively. All these movements were carried out without incident. With these changes, 'Plumer's Force' now had in the front line: the 27th and 28th Divisions, and the three infantry brigades of the 4th Division. In reserve were the three infantry brigades of the 50th Division, less two battalions of the 150th Brigade attached to the 11th Brigade, and the Canadian Division. On the morning of 2 May, Lieutenant-General Plumer issued orders for the next stage of the withdrawal. Unfortunately, before this could be initiated the Germans launched a gas attack, on a three-mile front, against the 4th Division, which held the line from Berlin Wood to Turco Farm. The gas cylinders, placed along the front from Locality C to the Ypres-Pilckem road, had been in position for some days but as was often the case, the wind direction was unfavourable, and the release had been postponed several times. The attack was started at midday with a heavy bombardment. During the afternoon, gas shells replaced high explosive and at 4.30 p.m. a cloud of chlorine gas was seen to move across No Man's Land, followed by men of the 51st and 53rd Reserve Divisions. The troops of the 12th Brigade were completely enveloped in the gas, and one battalion, the 2/Lancashire Fusiliers, was driven from its trench. It was so badly affected that eighteen officers and four hundred and thirty-one other ranks had to be hospitalised. Among those badly gassed was Private J Lynn, a battalion machine-gunner,

Turco Farm which was rebuilt on the original site.

who died the following day but was subsequently, awarded the Victoria Cross **(See chapter 5)**. The breach was immediately sealed by the 7/Argyll and Sutherland Highlanders together with a company of the 5/South Lancashire from the Brigade reserve. Although the Germans followed close behind the gas they were not quick enough to exploit the situation and were driven back without making any permanent gains. They also suffered badly under the artillery barrage, which was laid down on their lines, as soon as the gas was detected.

By 8.00 p.m. the situation had stabilised and all was quiet. So much so, that within two hours the order was given to execute the planned withdrawal. Although intermittent shelling continued throughout the night the withdrawal was successfully completed. All that now remained was to withdraw the infantry units back to the newly prepared line. Early the following day spasmodic shelling led to fears that the enemy might be about to renew his attack – possibly again aided by gas. But as the morning progressed and no attack materialised it was considered safe to issue orders for the final withdrawal. An attack was launched, in the vicinity of Berlin Wood in the afternoon, but by 9.00 p.m. it was deemed safe to proceed with the withdrawal. Under cover of a swirling ground mist all but the severely wounded were successfully moved back to the new trenches. The British Official History states:

> *With the successful completion of the retirement in the early morning of the 4th May, the phase of the fighting officially called the Battle of St. Julien closes. The German attacks in the battle of Ypres 1915 never had the weight or quality behind them that made those of October-November 1914 so dangerous. The enemy relied on overwhelming artillery superiority from a position of vantage on the high ground, and on the surprise of gas. The infantry forces that he employed were not formidable in numbers. But by an amazing piece of luck for him, coloured battalions and elderly third-line troops had just replaced a first-class French Division in the sector where he first elected to discharge the gas.*

His success in opening a gap was complete, but he made little use of the tremendous advantage he had gained, and his delay saved the situation for the allies.[2]

Edmonds is correct in saying that the Germans made little use of the advantage they had gained. But were they in position to do so? The answer is probably not. They were surprised that gas was so successful and probably did not realise how big a break they had made in the allied line. Gas was a new weapon to their senior officers and like many senior French and British officers, such men were slow to accept innovation. However, once gas had been used it was never again to be a surprise and the initial tactical advantage was lost. If they had been prepared, and willing, to follow up the attack of 22 April, Ypres could have fallen and the whole course of the war altered. In subsequent years, contrary to common belief, the Germans did not employ cloud gas to a large extent. By mid 1916 they ceased to use it altogether and relied instead on gas shells, filled with phosgene, mustard gas or respiratory irritant agents.

Sir John French's decision to sack Sir Horace Smith-Dorrien in the middle of the battle provoked much discussion. The enmity between the two men went back to before the beginning of the war. Both had served in South Africa, indeed, it was there that French established his reputation as a cavalry commander. Smith-Dorrien, on the other hand, was at first an infantry brigade commander and latterly in charge of a series of special 'columns', in which role he actually served under French. He left South Africa before the end of the war to go to India as Adjutant-General, a post he held from 1902 to 1903. French remained in South Africa until the Boers surrendered in May 1902, whereupon he returned to England. He had been appointed to command the 1st Army Corps at Aldershot, in place of his old chief Sir Redvers Buller He remained there until 1907. During his time at Aldershot French concentrated his attention very much on the *arme blanche* and left the other forces to their own devices. What changes were introduced into infantry training and procedures, based on the experiences of South Africa, occurred in spite of, rather than because of, the Commander-in-Chief. In 1907 French moved on, to become Inspector General of the Forces, and was succeeded by Smith-Dorrien. The new commander immediately instituted a new, less strictly controlled regime and implemented a number of changes to facilitate and improve infantry training. Alongside his military innovations he created excellent sporting facilities for off-duty soldiers, both officers and men. The changes infuriated French, who regarded them as being overt criticism of his Aldershot stewardship. Relations between the two deteriorated still further when, in 1909, Smith-Dorrien turned his attention to the cavalry. In Smith-Dorrien's view the cavalry training schemes still had far too much emphasis on appearance and on old-fashioned tactics, such as charges with lance and sabre. He insisted that all cavalrymen become competent in dismounted drill and in musketry. Sir John French was in no position to argue with these actions but his displeasure mounted and festered until 1914.

With the outbreak of war Field-Marshal Sir John French was appointed Commander-in Chief of the British Expeditionary Force with Lieutenant-General Sir Douglas Haig and Lieutenant-General Sir James Grierson as his two corps commanders. Unfortunately, Sir James Grierson had a heart attack, and died, on the train between Rouen and Amiens on 17 August. Sir John French immediately cabled Lord Kitchener requesting that Sir Herbert Plumer be sent as Grierson's replacement. Kitchener, whose ability as a staff officer had been seen to be sadly lacking in the South African campaign, ignored French's suggestion and replaced Grierson by Smith-Dorrien.

On the retreat from Mons, Smith-Dorrien being fearful for the fate of his corps, went against Sir John's wishes and fought the Battle of Le Cateau on 26 August. Sir John in his First Despatch, 7 September 1914, paid fulsome tribute to Sir Horace:

> *I cannot close the brief account of this glorious stand of the British troops without putting on record my deep appreciation of the valuable services rendered by General Sir Horace Smith-Dorrien.*

> *I say without hesitation that the saving of the left wing of my command on the morning of the 26th August could never have been accomplished unless a commander of rare and unusual coolness, intrepidity, and determination had been present to personally conduct the operation.*[3]

By 1916 Sir John French had himself been replaced, as Commander-in-Chief, by Sir Douglas Haig. In 1917 following the publication of 'The Retreat from Mons' by Major Corbett-Smith, which contained criticism of his actions, Sir John enlisted the help of a 'Times' newspaper journalist, Lovat Fraser, to produce his own book *'1914'*. He did not make reference to the dismissal of Sir Horace in 1915 but took the opportunity to revise the statement quote above:

> *The superb gallantry of the troops and the skilful leading by Divisional and Brigade Commanders, helped very materially by the support given by Allenby and as I afterwards learned by*

Sordet and d'Amade, saved the 2nd Corps...the actual result was a total loss of at least 14,000 officers and men, about 80 guns, numbers of machine guns, as well as quantities of ammunition.

The effect upon the British Army was to render the subsequent conduct of the retreat more difficult and arduous.

In my despatch, written in September 1914, I refer eulogistically to the Battle of Le Cateau. I had been, together with my staff, directing the movements of the British Army day and night up to the time of the Battle of the Marne – in the course of which battle I received an urgent demand from the Government that a despatch should be forwarded.

It was completed, of necessity, very hurriedly, and before there had been time to study the reports immediately preceding and covering the period of the battle, by which alone the full details could be disclosed.

It was, indeed, impossible, until much later on, to appreciate in all its details the actual situation on the morning of 26th August. [4]

In later sections he went on to accuse Smith-Dorrien of abject pessimism at the end of September and during the First Battle of Ypres.

Before the book was published, extracts appeared in 'The Daily Telegraph'. A furore followed, in which the right of Sir John French to publish the book was questioned – he was still technically a serving officer. At the same time Sir Horace demanded a right to reply, which on the advice of the Chief of the Imperial General Staff, Sir Henry Wilson, the government refused. Left with no other choice Sir Horace produced, and circulated privately, a sixty page 'Statement with regard to Lord French's Book "1914"'.

Even at the time of publication Sir John's version of events was dismissed by many of his contemporaries. History has been no less critical and many present day historians would agree that Smith-Dorrien was the victim of an unjust and malicious attack.

A copy of Smith-Dorrien's original publication can be found in the Public Record Office. [5] However, Professor Ian Beckett has also produced the full text, together with an introduction, in his book 'The Judgement of History'. [6]

Bibliography

1. *War Diary II Army. General Staff*. Public Record Office. WO95/270.
2. *Military Operations in France & Belgium*. 1915 Volume 1. Edmonds. Macmillan 1927.
3. *The Despatches of Sir John French*. Chapman & Hall. London 1917.
4. *1914*. Sir John French. Constable and Co. London. 1919.
5. Public Record Office. CAB 45/206.
6. *The Judgement of History*. I F W Beckett. Tom Donovan. London 1993.

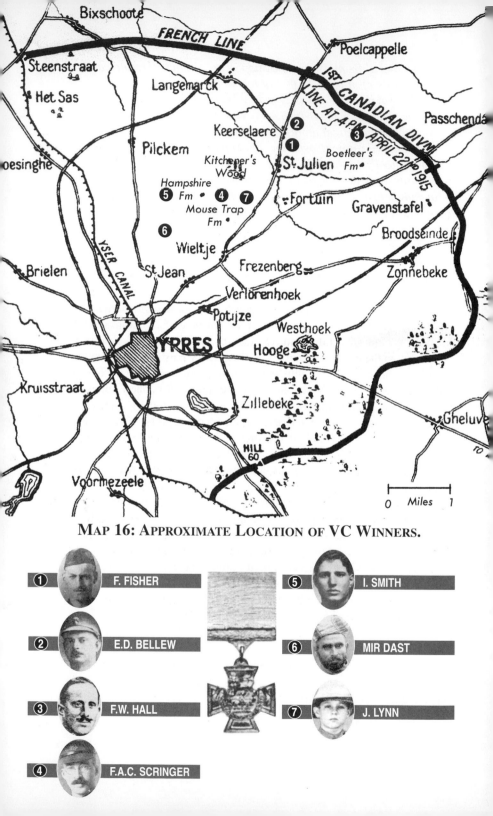

MAP 16: APPROXIMATE LOCATION OF VC WINNERS.

1 F. FISHER

2 E.D. BELLEW

3 F.W. HALL

4 F.A.C. SCRINGER

5 I. SMITH

6 MIR DAST

7 J. LYNN

Chapter Five

RECIPIENTS OF THE VICTORIA CROSS

During the period of the Second Battle of Ypres, covered by this volume, a total of seven Victoria Crosses were awarded. Of these: four were won by members of the Canadian 1st Division, two by members of the Lahore Division and one by a member of the British 4th Division **(See map 16 page 94)**.

Frederick Fisher

As the French and Canadian troops fought to combat the appalling effects of the first gas attack they were aided by the 10th Battery Canadian Field Artillery **(See map 7 page 33)**. The battery, located some 500 yards north of St. Julien and to the east of the Keerselare road, opened fire at about 5.45 p.m. on the German first line trenches. As the stream of choking French colonial troops fled back through the gun lines a large body of the enemy was sighted away to the west. They were already moving south but were still well within the range of the 10th Battery's guns. Major W B King, the battery commander, immediately ordered one section to reverse its guns and engage the enemy. As the first shots fell among them, the Germans fell to earth and, proceeded to dig themselves in. Major King called to the infantry for a covering party to be sent forward. In response a mixed party, of the 14th and 15th Battalions, was sent forward from its position in St. Julien, commanded by Lieutenant G W Stairs of the 14th Battalion. Included in the party was Lance Corporal Fred Fisher, 13th Battalion, in charge of a Colt machine-gun. Showing great skill and determination, Lance Corporal Fisher managed to make his way forward to the shelter of an isolated building. Here, he set up his gun, brought it to bear and stopped any further movement by the enemy. During the rest of the evening he covered the withdrawal of the battery to safer ground. For this action he was awarded the Victoria Cross. During the action he lost four of his gun-team but undaunted returned to St. Julien, where he called for volunteers to return with him to the line. He was to be killed the following day while attempting to set up his gun in the 13th Battalion's lines.

The award was recorded in the London Gazette, No. 29202, dated 22 June 1915. The citation gives the date of the action as the 23 April 1915 but this is incorrect. It was on this day that he was killed. Lance Corporal Fisher's body was not recovered and he is commemorated on the Menin Gate Memorial to the Missing at Ypres. He was the first Canadian born man to win the Victoria Cross while serving in the Canadian Army

Frederick Fisher was born on 3 August 1894 in St. Catherine's, Ontario, Canada, the fourth of four children. He was educated in a series of Public Schools in Canada, his attendance at which followed the movement of his father, from post to post, in his profession as a banker. In 1912 'Bud', as he was generally known, enrolled as a student at McGill University to read engineering. His course was still unfinished when, in August 1914, he enlisted as a private in the 5th Regiment (Royal Highlanders of Canada). After initial training at Valcartier Camp, Quebec, the 13th Battalion was shipped to England for further training on Salisbury Plain. The unit finally landed in France in early February 1915, by which time Fisher had been promoted to Lance Corporal.

His Victoria Cross was sent to his parents in August 1915 and worn by his mother at a ceremony at McGill University on the 25 April 1916, when a portrait of the ex-student was unveiled.

Edward Bellew

Following the renewed attack by the enemy, on 24 April, on the Canadian line between Kitchener's Wood and Locality C a hurried meeting between the commanders of the Canadian 7th, 14th and 15th Battalions took place at the Enfiladed Cross Roads **(See chapter 3 & map 12 page 56)**. As a result of this meeting the Canadians reluctantly decided on a withdrawal to a position covering Fortuin. In the course of this withdrawal the progress of the enemy was impeded by the valour of Lieutenant Edward Donald Bellew, machine-gun officer of the 7th Battalion. Lieutenant Bellew had positioned his gun team on the high ground to the north of St. Julien, overlooking Keerselare **(See map 16 page 94)** His trained gunners were soon hit so he took over the handling of one gun himself whilst the other was in the hands of a sergeant. Although it was obvious to the defenders that the task was hopeless they continued to harass the enemy. Eventually the sergeant was killed and Lieutenant Bellew was severely wounded. Nevertheless, he got up and continued to fire until all his ammunition was spent. The enemy then rushed the position and Bellew was taken prisoner. During his imprisonment he was twice tried on a charge that he continued to fire after a surrender had been accepted. At the end of the second trial he was acquitted. He remained a prisoner until, due to ill health, he was first moved to an internment camp in Switzerland before being repatriated to England in December 1918. He was promoted to the rank of Captain on 2 January 1916.

Although the extent of his bravery was well known in 1915, no announcement of the award of the Victoria Cross was made until 1919, probably as a consequence of his imprisonment. The citation in the London Gazette, No. 31340, dated 15 May 1919, named the sergeant involved as Sergeant Peerless. However, the Commonwealth War Graves Commission records show no Sergeant Peerless killed that day but do record the death of Sergeant Hugh Nisbet Pearless 7th Battalion Canadian Infantry on 24 April 1915. He was the son of Mr and Mrs R W Pearless of Worthing, Sussex, England. Sergeant Pearless, who was awarded the DCM in June 1915, has no known grave but is commemorated on Menin Gate Memorial to the Missing at Ypres.

Edward Bellew was the eldest son of Major Patrick Bellew of the Bengal Army. He was born on 28 October 1882, possibly on the High Seas, but more likely at Malabar Hill, Bombay. In common with many sons of Indian officers he was educated in England and followed his father, grandfather and great-grandfather into the army. On his graduation from Sandhurst he was commissioned into the Royal Irish Regiment in May 1901. He only remained with the regiment for two years, leaving as a Lieutenant, in August 1903.

He emigrated to Canada in 1907, and joined the Canadian Army on 10 August 1914. He left Valcartier Camp with the 7th Battalion on 3 October 1914 and disembarked at Plymouth on 16 October. After a period on Salisbury Plain the 7th Battalion finally landed in France in mid February 1915. After his release he returned to Canada, where he died on 1 February 1961.

Frederick Hall

At almost the same time as Lieutenant Bellew was holding out against impossible odds, away to his right, Company-Sergeant Major F W Hall was also gaining the highest honour of his country **(See map 16 page 94)**. After the initial withdrawal, agreed to at the meeting of

Colour-Sergeant Hall falls mortally wounded in attempting the rescue a wounded comrade.

commanders at Enfiladed Cross Roads, a further meeting, this time including Major Ormond of the 10th Battalion, saw no alternative but to continue the withdrawal to the Gravenstafel-Wieltje road. This action led to the creation of a gap in the line between Locality C and the 2nd Brigade. The only troops in this gap were two battalions of the 8th Battalion north of Boetleer's Farm. Although the order to withdraw had been issued, Lieutenant-Colonel Lipsett, still mindful of his earlier order to protect Locality C, decided to move up his last reserves in an attempt to plug the gap on his left flank. When these reserves, two platoons C Company, moved towards the gap, the officer in charge was almost immediately killed and Company-Sergeant Major Hall took over. He led them over a high bank, which was swept by rifle and machine-gun fire, and gained a position in the front line. On looking back, he saw several wounded men and immediately climbed back out of the trench and retraced his steps. In two forays he brought in two men, one after the other. Later he became aware of a third wounded man and together with two volunteers, Corporal Payne and Private Rogerson, again went back over the parados. His two companions were almost immediately hit and all three were forced to return to the safety of the trench. Shortly, Hall again went out. This time he managed to reach the man and having picked him up started back when he was hit in the head and mortally wounded. For this courageous act Company-Sergeant Major Hall was awarded the Victoria Cross, the citation for which, appeared in the London Gazette, No. 29202, dated 23 June 1915. Frederick Hall has no known grave but he is commemorated on Menin Gate Memorial to the Missing at Ypres.

Frederic William Hall was born in Kilkenny, Ireland, on 8 February 1885, the son of Bombardier and Mrs F Hall. He enlisted in the Cameronians (Scottish Rifles) and served for just over twelve years before emigrating to Canada in 1910. At the outbreak of war he enlisted in the 106th Regiment (Winnipeg Light Infantry) but later transferred to the 8th Battalion Canadian Infantry. In common with members of other Canadian units he trained at Valcartier Camp before being moved to Salisbury Plain in England. By February 1915 he had been twice promoted: to acting sergeant in October and to Colour-Sergeant in December 1914. He sailed for France on 10 February 1915.

Francis Alexander Scrimger

In the afternoon of 25 April, after the second gas attack, the Advanced Dressing Station of the 3rd Canadian Field Ambulance, in the outhouses of Brigadier-General Turner's headquarters at Mouse Trap Farm **(See map 16 page 94)**, came under intense artillery fire. Indeed, the farm had been subject to almost continuous fire, of one sort or another, since the attack on 22 April. The station was under the command of Captain Francis Alexander Caron Scrimger, Canadian Army Medical Service, Medical Officer of the 14th Battalion Canadian Infantry. Conditions in the farm were chaotic, with many men already awaiting treatment and more arriving, in a continuous stream, from the front. By late afternoon the situation became so bad, with many of the buildings on fire, that evacuation of the site became imperative. As the wounded were carried out, one man, Captain Harold MacDonald, Brigadier-General Turner's Brigade Captain, was in danger of being left behind. Seeing his plight, Captain Scrimger picked him up and carried him out through the hail of fire and took refuge in the water of the moat. Here, he protected the injured officer with his own body until stretcher-bearers found them and removed Captain MacDonald to safety.

The award of the Victoria Cross to Captain Scrimger was announced in the London Gazette, No. 29202, dated 22 June 1915. In the citation it was made clear that the award was made, not only for

Captain Scrimger's treatment of Captain MacDonald, but for his devotion to duty and to his patients throughout the period of the three days 22-25 April 1915.

Francis Scrimger was born in Montreal, on 10 February 1881, the son of the Reverend John Scrimger, a senior Presbyterian Minister. From school, he entered McGill University Medical School, graduating in 1905. After further training he joined the Canadian Army Medical Corps in 1912 and with the advent of war was appointed Medical Officer of the 14th Battalion Canadian Infantry.

After his award Captain Scrimger continued in the medical service reaching, by April 1919, the rank of Lieutenant-Colonel. He subsequently returned to Canada and worked in the Royal Victoria Hospital, Montreal, until his death in February 1937.

Issy Smith (Ishroulch Shmeilowitz)

When, on 26 April 1915, the Lahore Division attacked **(See maps 13 & 16 pages 77 & 94)**, it did so with the Jullundur Brigade on the right and the Ferozepore Brigade on the left. As the two brigades moved across Hill Top ridge towards Hill Top Farm, the 1/Manchester, on the extreme right of the Jullundur Brigade, were cut down by heavy enemy fire. Acting Corporal Issy Smith had already been fortunate to escape unhurt when a stray shell hit his platoon on its way up to the start line. Now pinned down in a trench, some way from the enemy line, he could see numbers of his comrades who, having got further forward, were wounded and trapped out in the open. With complete disregard for his own safety Smith went out and brought back a number of the wounded, some from as far as 250 yards. The announcement of the award of the Victoria Cross was made in the London Gazette, No. 29272, dated 23 August 1915.

Ishroulch Shmeilowitz, Issy Smith, was the son of French parents of Polish decent. He was born in 1890 and by 1904 was living in England where he enlisted in the army. He served with the 1st Battalion, Manchester Regiment, until his discharge in 1912. He then moved to Australia but was back in England late in 1914 and rejoined the 1/Manchester via the 3rd Battalion. After the receipt of the Victoria Cross, the second of the war to be won by a member of the Jewish faith, he was gassed in May of the same year and sent to a hospital in Dublin. He was finally presented with his Victoria Cross by King George V, at Buckingham Palace, on 3 February 1916. Demobilised in

Issy Smith rescuing a wounded man.

1919, having reached the rank of sergeant, he had various jobs in London before returning to Australia in 1928. By this time he was married with a daughter and within two years had become a Justice of the Peace in Melbourne. He died in Australia in September 1940 and was buried in a Jewish cemetery in Victoria, with full military honours.

Mir Dast

When the combined effects of the enemy fire and chlorine gas halted the attack by the Ferozepore Brigade on 26 April, the troops were forced to fall back in search of cover. Jemadar Mir Dast, 55th Coke's Rifles, attached to the 57th Rifles, remained behind after all his officers had been either killed or wounded **(See map 16 page 94)**. As the effects of the gas began to wear off, Mir Dast worked tirelessly to steady the men and kept them together until, after dusk, he received orders to retire. In the course of the retirement he came across a number of men who had found cover in old trenches and these he led to safety. He then returned into the open and assisted in bringing in eight wounded British and Indian Officers. In the course of this splendid effort he was himself wounded. One of the men he helped to safety was Havildar Mangal Singh, who had been rendered unconscious by the gas. When he recovered consciousness he in turn went out to bring in more wounded. For his actions Jemadar Mir

Mir Dast VC leading his platoon in the Lahore Division attack.

Dast was awarded the Victoria Cross, the award of which was announced in the London Gazette, No. 29210, dated 29 June 1915. He was the fourth Indian soldier to receive that honour. Havildar Mangal Singh was awarded the Indian Order of Merit, Second Class.

Mir Dast was born in Maiden, Tirah, India, on 3 December 1874. Aged 20, he enlisted in Coke's Rifles and saw service in several trouble spots including the north-west frontier. By 1914 he had been promoted to the rank of Jemadar (Lieutenant) and had received several awards for bravery including, what at the time was the highest Indian award, the Indian Order of Merit. He arrived in France in 1915, in time for the battle of Neuve Chapelle but was not seriously involved. When his award was announced, in June 1915, Mir Dast was already in England, having again been wounded. King George V presented him with his medal, in the grounds of the Indian Hospital, in the Royal Pavilion, Brighton on 25 August 1915. In September 1917, his health having not sufficiently recovered, he was removed from the active service list. However, by this time he had been further decorated, making him one of the most highly decorated Indian soldiers. He died in what is know Pakistan in 1945.

At the time of Mir Dast's award an interesting story was circulated. Mir Dast had a brother, Mir Mast also serving as a Jamadar, in Vaughan's Rifles. In early March he and eight other Indian soldiers deserted to the enemy near Neuve Chapelle. To add insult to injury the Indian Corps was devastated to hear that the Kaiser had rewarded Mir Mast with the Iron Cross. The Corps and regimental honour was partially restored by Mir Dast. However, there appears to be no documentary evidence to either support or deny the story.

John Lynn

At midday on 2 May the Germans launched an attack on a three-mile front between Berlin Wood and Turco Farm. The attack culminated, at 1.30 p.m., in the release of chlorine gas across the line held by the British 12th Brigade (Brigadier-General F G Anley), 4th Division, between Fortuin and Turco Farm. The 2/Lancashire Fusiliers (Lieutenant-Colonel C J Griffith), in front of Mouse Trap Farm, were not given sufficient warning to don their improvised respirators and were driven from their trench, suffering heavy gas casualties. The battalion possessed four machine-guns and one of these, under Private John Lynn, was located behind a bank just west of the Wieltje-St. Julien road **(See map 16 page 94)**. As the thick fog of gas rolled over the front Private Lynn placed his gun on top of the parapet and swept the area, in and behind the green gas, with murderous machine gun fire. He continued to take toll of the advancing enemy until, overcome by the gas, he collapsed. When the situation had been stabilised, Private Lynn was given medical treatment but died, in hospital, the following day. His award of the Victoria Cross was announced in the London Gazette, No. 29210, dated 29 June 1915.

John Lynn was born in 1887 and was fostered by Mr & Mrs Harrison of Forest Hill London. In 1901 he enlisted in the 4th Battalion Lancashire Fusiliers but later served with the 2nd Battalion of the same regiment. He left the army but, being on the reserve, was recalled when war was declared. The 2nd Battalion Lancashire Fusiliers sailed for France, from Southampton, on 22 August and landed at Boulogne the following day. In mid-October the battalion was engaged in operations around Le Touquet (near Ploegsteert) where Private Lynn was awarded the Distinguished Conduct Medal for his work in the machine-gun section. The battalion remained in the line throughout the winter. After his death Private Lynn was also awarded the Russian Cross of St. George, 4th Class. He was buried in Vlamertinghe but the grave was later lost. He is now commemorated on a special Vlamertinghe Churchyard Memorial in Grootebeek British Cemetery, Reninghelst.

The commemorative stone of Private J Lynn VC in Grootebeek Cemetery, Reninghelst.

Grootebeek Cemetery Reninghelst.

Map 17. Battlefield Car Tour No. 1.

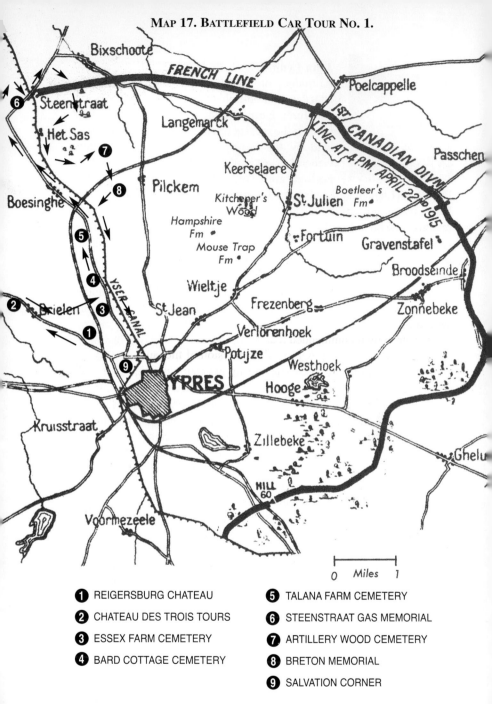

1. REIGERSBURG CHATEAU
2. CHATEAU DES TROIS TOURS
3. ESSEX FARM CEMETERY
4. BARD COTTAGE CEMETERY
5. TALANA FARM CEMETERY
6. STEENSTRAAT GAS MEMORIAL
7. ARTILLERY WOOD CEMETERY
8. BRETON MEMORIAL
9. SALVATION CORNER

Chapter Six

BATTLEFIELD TOURS

Introduction

The main sites of interest in the actions occurring over the period 22 April 1915 to 3 May 1915, are spread over quite a wide area. The two road tours suggested below cover the eastern and western sides respectively, and include memorials and cemeteries where appropriate. With regard to the battlefield walks St Julien does not lend itself to the use of footpaths and agricultural tracks in the way that can be done on the Somme. The tracks simply do not exist. However, good coverage can be achieved using the many minor roads in the area. Most of these roads were reinstated, after the war, in positions very close to their original lines, as can be judged by comparing the current positions with those on trench maps.

It is strongly recommended that the road tours be carried out before embarking on the walks. A general impression of the land can then be reinforced by closer examination. Indeed, for many people the overall view may be sufficient. A number of cemeteries will be encountered on the way round but not all of these contain burials relevant to the period under consideration. However, where the cemetery is deemed to be of interest descriptions have been included. The cemeteries also provide excellent stopping points, usually with space to get the car off the road and, sometimes, good vantage points to assess the lie of the land.

As stated in the earlier section, Advice to Travellers, good Belgian maps are difficult to obtain so the French IGN 1: 100,000 No. 2, Lille-Dunkerque is recommended. In addition a street map of Ypres could be found to be useful. A good one, produced by 'Geocart', is available from newsagents in Ypres. Not only does it contain a street map of the city but also a larger map showing roads out as far as Langemarck and Steenstraat.

Car tour No. 1: The Eastern side of the Battlefield

Map: IGN No. 2, Lille-Dunkerque   **Map 17.**

Leave the Grote Markt by J. Coomansstraat, which runs behind the Cloth Hall in front of the Belgian War Memorial and continue down

The grave of Colonel A D Geddes in Ypres Reservoir Cemetery.

Vandepeereboomplein past St Martin's Cathedral. Turn left into Elverdingsestraat passing St George's Memorial Church on the left-hand side. At the crossroads turn right into the N 8, M. Haiglaan, signposted to Veurne, Diksmuide and Poperinghe. Shortly, on the right hand side, there is a Commonwealth War Graves Commission green signpost to **Ypres Reservoir Cemetery**. A short detour to the cemetery, along M. Plumerlaan, is worthwhile. The cemetery was begun in October 1915 and was used until after the Armistice. It then contained 1,099 graves; it now contains over 2,500, resulting from the concentration of burials from smaller cemeteries. Among those buried in the cemetery is Colonel A D Geddes, commander of Geddes's Detachment, who was killed on 28 April 1915. His grave reference is Plot IV, Row C, 4. An interesting group of graves is to be found in Plot V, Row AA. These graves are those of officers and men of the 6th Duke of Cornwall's Light Infantry who were billeted in the vaults of the cathedral and were killed on 12th August 1915 by a large shell fired from Houthulst Forest. Their bodies were not recovered until after the war ended.

Return to the main road, or continue along the road if you have not visited Ypres Reservoir Cemetery, to cross the route of the old railway, which ran from Ypres to Staden. This line will be crossed several times in the course of this tour. Pass Reigersburg Chateau on the right hand side of the road, which was an artillery base for much of the war, and continue across the N 38 to reach Brielen. Drive through the centre, and as you leave, on the left hand side of the road, opposite the Brielen sign, a wood hides the rebuilt Chateau des Trois Tours. A private road

The Chateau des Trois Tours.

leads down to the chateau, which was the headquarters of the Canadian Division during the fighting around St. Julien. Continue to reach the Café de Krikke, which provides a good point at which to turn round. When doing so set the car to face the ground directly across the road from the café. Several farm buildings are visible. They are the rebuilt farms which during the war were given names, probably by the French, derived from Napoleon Bonaparte's battles: Leipzig, on the left, Jena, in the centre, and Austerlitz, on the right.

Return to Brielen and at the exit sign turn left into Noordhofweg (if you reach the main N 38 road you have gone too far!). Approximately half a mile along the road it was crossed by the Ypres-Staden railway line. On the left hand side of the road are two further farms which bore names associated with Napoleon. Adjacent to the road is Kleber Farm and further back Murat Farm, named after two of his Marshals. It is understandable that such names should have been used as the ground, in which they were located, was controlled by the Groupement d'Elverdinghe.

Continue past the farms to reach a T-junction and **Essex Farm Cemetery**. It is worthwhile to stop here to visit the memorial to Colonel John McCrae, who wrote the well-known poem *In Flanders Fields*, which stands just outside the cemetery. Nearby are bunkers, recently restored, which formed part of an Advanced Dressing Station. The cemetery was started in April 1915 and continued in use until August 1917. Plot No. I contains dead of the 49th (West Riding) Division whose memorial stands on the canal bank, behind the cemetery. This Division suffered many casualties in the first phosgene gas attack in December 1915. Among other burials is V J Strudwick of the Rifle Brigade, reference Plot I, Row U, 8. who died on 14 January 1916 aged only 15 years, and is therefore, one of the youngest of the war's casualties. Also buried here is Private T Barratt, 7th Battalion South Staffordshire Regiment, reference Plot I, Row Z, 8. who was awarded a posthumous Victoria Cross for his gallantry on the day he died (27 July 1917). He was detailed to act as scout to a patrol. As he approached the enemy lines he came under fire from a number of snipers whom he stalked and killed. When the patrol endeavoured to regain its own lines a party of Germans was observed, moving to cut them off. Private Barratt immediately volunteered to cover the retirement, which he did, causing many enemy casualties. On reaching his own lines he was killed by a shell.

A walk down the track to the canal will bring you to the site of Bridge No. 4, the Brielen Bridge, over the canal. After the breakthrough by the Germans on 22 April 1915, units of the Canadian Field Artillery occupied the ground around Essex Farm.

Return to the T-junction and from the road upon which you reached Essex Farm turn left into the N 369 Dikesmuidseweg. This road runs parallel with the canal towards Boesinghe (Boezinge). On the left hand side of the road is **Bard Cottage Cemetery**. Named after a house set back from the line, the cemetery was used between June 1915 and October 1918. It contains burials from the 49th (West Riding) Division and 38th (Welsh) Division, who also served in this area. Further on, also on the left-hand side of the road, is **Talana Farm Cemetery**. It was started by French Zouaves in April 1915 but taken over by the British in the following June. It was named, along with several nearby farms, after actions in the Boer War 1899-1902. Colenso Farm is directly opposite the cemetery on the other side of the road. Continue on the road to by-pass Boesinghe. The western edge of the gas cloud on 22 April reached Boesinghe and spread out across the road to the Northwest. The German front line at midnight on the 22nd ran almost parallel with the road on the other side of the canal. When roads join bear left on the one signposted: Reninge, Noordschote and Zuidscote. Stop at the next crossroads and note the Demarcation Stone on the left-hand corner. Opposite the stone, on the side of the corner shop, is a blue plate. This plate bears the name of General Lodz, commanding the French Regiment of Grenadiers in April 1915, and has an arrow pointing to the Grenadier Memorial. Go straight ahead at the crossroads and the Grenadier Memorial can soon be seen on the right hand side. Take the next turning, on the right, to reach the memorial, which bears a plaque commemorating the resistance of the Grenadiers during the first German gas attack.

Continue along the road to reach a T-junction with Dikesmuidseweg. As you do so you should see a white memorial almost directly in front of you. This will be visited later in the tour. At the junction, on the right hand side, is the Steenstraat Memorial to the first victims of asphyxiating gas. The present memorial, erected after the Second World War, replaced the original large stone one, which was destroyed by the Germans, who objected to the inscription. It was one of the few First World War memorials to be destroyed by the Germans during the

French Memorial to the Officers and Men of the 3° Regiment de Ligne who died in April and May 1915, Steenstraat.

The original Steenstraat memorial which was destroyed during the Second World War. J BRAZIER COLLECTION

Second War. Note the small lamp in an alcove near the base of the memorial. It is often hidden by poppies or other flowers.

Turn left at the junction, into Dikesmuidseweg, and stop just in front of the canal bridge to visit the white French Memorial seen earlier. It bears an inscription commemorating 162 French soldiers who fell at Steenstraat breaking the German offensive after the first release of gas. Cross the canal and take the second turning on the right, Zuidschotestraat and then shortly right again into Poezelstraat. At the crossroads turn right again into Sasstraat and follow the road to Het Sas lock. It was here that the German 46th

The replacement memorial to the victims of asphyxiating gas.

The lock at Het Sas where the German troops crossed on 22 April, 1915.

Reserve Division managed to cross the canal on 22 April. Continue down the road and where it bends sharply to the left was the point where the German line crossed back over the canal. At the T-junction, turn left then first right to rejoin Poezelstraat and stop at **Artillery Wood Cemetery** on the right-hand side. Buried in this cemetery is Captain John Pixley, 4th Battalion Grenadier Guards, who was killed in action on 12 October 1917. His grave reference is Plot XI, Row C, 5. Subsequently, in 1928, his sister Olive Pixley, published a short account of her psychical experiences concerning her dead brother. The story 'Listening In' has recently been republished by IMCC Ltd.

Continue down Poezelstraat, yet again crossing the line of the old Ypres-Staden railway, to reach the Breton Memorial, 'Carrefour de la Rose'. Turn right and stop in front of the memorial, which is an authentic Breton Calvary, many of which can still be found in the Breton countryside. It was brought here, from Brittany, to commemorate the men from that part of France who suffered in the first gas attack. Continue along the road in front of the memorial and take the second turning on the left Oostkaai, signposted Ieper 5, which runs along the side the canal. The bridges across the canal, referred to in Chapter 2, were situated along this part of the canal, as mentioned earlier at Essex Farm. The land on the left hand side of the road has now been largely developed for industry, but some of the access roads bear names referring back to the farms, such as the two Zwaanhofs, which stood there in 1915. At the end of the canal, Salvation Corner, turn left into Polenlaan and return to the Grote Markt by following signs to Centrum.

Total distance approximately 20 miles.

Breton 'Carrefour de la Rose' Memorial, Boesinghe with dedication.

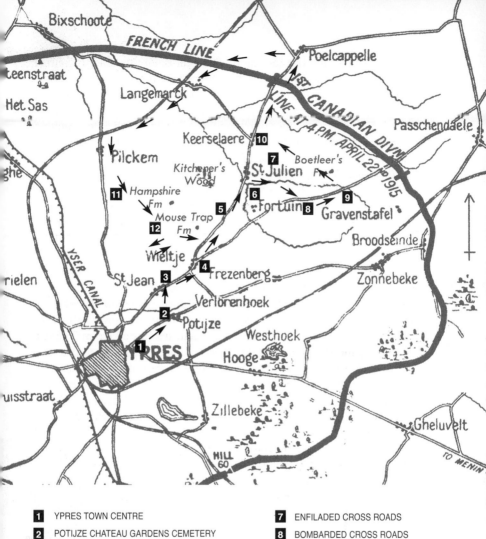

1	YPRES TOWN CENTRE		**7**	ENFILADED CROSS ROADS
2	POTIJZE CHATEAU GARDENS CEMETERY		**8**	BOMBARDED CROSS ROADS
3	WIELTJE FARM CEMETERY		**9**	BERLIN WOOD
4	BRITISH 50TH DIV MEMORIAL		**10**	VANCOUVER CORNER
5	SEAFORTH (CHEDDAR VILLA) CEMETERY		**11**	NO MAN'S COT CEMETERY
6	ST JULIEN D.S. CEMETERY		**12**	TRACK 'X' CEMETERY

Car tour No. 2: The Western Side of the Battlefield

Map: IGN No. 2, Lille-Dunkerque   **Map 18.**

Leave the Grote Markt by the Menin Gate. It is not possible to drive
directly to the gate from the square owing to the one-way system. Take

St. Jacobstraat, the last turning on the right before the one-way street to the gate. Pass the church on the left and take the next turning on the left, Moskoustraat. At the end turn left again and continue to the Menin Gate. Turn right through the gate and take the N 332 and pass **Ypres Town Cemetery** on the right-hand side of the road. On reaching Potijze go straight over the roundabout to visit three cemeteries associated with Potijze Chateau, which was the British 27th Division headquarters. All three cemeteries are to be found on the left-hand side of the road. Two, **Potijze Chateau Grounds** and **Potijze Chateau Lawn** are adjacent to the road but the third, **Potijze Chateau Wood**, is somewhat back from it. Potijze was within the British lines for the whole of the war. The chateau contained an Advance Dressing Station but even so was subject to incessant artillery fire and eventually destroyed. All three cemeteries were started early in 1915 and used either continuously or at intervals until 1918.

Return to the Potijze roundabout and turn right into Potyzestraat and pass **Potijze Burial Ground Cemetery**. At the crossroads in St. Jean (Sint-Jan) turn right into N 313 and shortly arrive at **Wieltje Farm Cemetery**. Take the turning on the right-hand side of the road bearing a Commonwealth War Graves Commission signpost to **Oxford Road Cemetery**. Oxford road was the name given to a road running behind the support trenches, from a point west of the village of Wieltje to the Potijze-Zonnebeke road. The cemetery was not started until late in the war in 1917. Continue past the cemetery to reach the 50th (Northumbrian) Division Memorial. When unveiled in 1929, by Field Marshal Lord Plumer, there was a path from the gate leading up to the plinth, which is no longer in place. Bear left to pass under the bridge, then turn left and right to rejoin the N 313 Roeselarestraat signposted to Poelkapelle. Shortly join N 38 Brugseweg and continue to reach **Seaforth Cemetery**, **Cheddar Villa** on the right hand side of the road. On the 25 and 26 April 1915 there was severe fighting in this vicinity; the British dead were buried on the spot. The cemetery was originally

The 50th Northumberland Division Memorial at Oxford Road.

Cheddar Villa bunker at the end of the war.

called Cheddar Villa but was changed in 1922 at the request of the 2nd Seaforth Highlanders, as there are many dead from this unit in the cemetery. Note the remains of a large bunker incorporated into the adjacent farm. On the other side of the road, past a few smaller houses, is the rebuilt Vanheule Farm. Continue on towards St. Julien (St. Juliaan) and on entering the village a Commonwealth War Graves Commission sign indicates the position of **St. Julien Dressing Station Cemetery**. Take the road down to the cemetery and park in front of it. When so parked the ground in front to the left is that known as Fortuin (Fortuinhoek). Return to the main road and turn right into the village and then right again and immediately left to pass the church and cemetery. The first set of crossroads encountered, with a windmill at 11 o'clock, is Enfiladed Cross Roads. Turn right and continue to reach Bombarded Cross Roads. It was at these two road junctions that the Canadian battalion commanders conferred on the morning of 24 April 1915 **(See Chapter 2)**. At the second set of crossroads turn left into Roeslarestraat signposted to the New Zealand Memorial. Cross the next junction, passing the New Zealand Memorial, and shortly Berlin Wood can be seen on the right-hand side of the road. The junction between the Canadian Division and the British 28th Division lay on the front edge of the wood. On 22 April the ground to the right of the road was held by the British 85th Brigade and that to the left by the Canadian 2nd Brigade. When, on the 26 April, the enemy broke through in this sector the German line ran along the road from Gravenstafel back to Bombarded Cross Roads and then along the road towards Enfiladed Cross Roads. However, before reaching the Enfiladed Cross Roads it dropped back into the ground to the left of the road. If you drive a little further along the road, in the direction of

The Brooding Soldier Memorial, Vancouver Corner.

Gravenstafel, **Tyne Cot Cemetery** and Passchendaele church can be seen beyond Berlin Wood.

Turn round and go back to the New Zealand Memorial and there turn right into Schipstraat. Where the road bends Boetleer's Farm can be seen on the right-hand side of the road. It was in the ground above the farm and in front of the Stroombeke that C.S.M. Hall won the Victoria Cross. Continue along the road to pass through Locality C before taking the road on the left-hand side back to the Enfiladed Cross Roads. Turn right up to Vancouver Corner and the Brooding Soldier Canadian Memorial where there is ample car parking space. In the ground to your left, as you drive from Enfiladed Cross Roads to Vancouver Corner, Lance Corporal Fisher won his Victoria Cross, and the 10th Battery, Canadian Field Artillery held up the enemy advance. The memorial marks the battlefield where 18,000 Canadians on the British left withstood the first German gas attacks on 22 and 24 April 1915. It is a very moving memorial showing a soldier with head bowed leaning on

THIS·COLUMN·MARKS·THE BATTLEFIELD·WHERE·18,000 CANADIANS·ON·THE·BRITISH LEFT·WITHSTOOD·THE·FIRST GERMAN·GAS·ATTACKS·THE 22-24·APRIL·1915·2,000·FELL AND·LIE·BURIED·NEARBY

Canadans cheered after their great stand at St Julien, April 1915, by the relieving West Kents.

The Lekkerboterbeek between St. Julien and Poelcappelle.

reversed arms. At night it is illuminated following an agreement between the Canadian Government, which paid for the installation, and the local community, which meets the running costs.

If you wish the tour can be terminated at this point by joining the N 313 and returning directly to Ypres. Alternatively turn right towards Keerselare. In the ground to the right Lieutenant Bellew won his Victoria Cross. Continue towards Poelcappelle and shortly cross over the Lekkerboterbeek. Between this point and Poelcappelle the two front lines, on 22 April, crossed the road. The junction between the French and Canadian troops was about two hundred yards to the right of the road, so it was the French who held the line on the road. In Poelcappelle note the memorial to the French air ace Georges Guynemer, who was killed on 11 September 1917 when he crashed in the vicinity of the village. The stork on the memorial was the emblem of Guynemer's squadron and is said to be flying in the direction taken by Guynemer on the day he died. The memorial was unveiled in 1923. There are several cafés in the village, which therefore provides an excellent stopping place.

Guynemer Memorial, Poelcappelle.

Starting from the road on which you entered the village, take the fourth exit from the roundabout, to Langemarck. Approximately half way to Langemarck the road was crossed by the two front lines, which extended north-westwards from the St. Julien-Poelcappelle road. On reaching Langemarck turn right at the traffic lights with directions to the Langemarck German Cemetery. If you have not visited a German cemetery the one at Langemarck is very

115

evocative. Pass by the square to reach the German Cemetery on the left-hand side of the road. Langemarck is also a good stop for refreshments. Try 'de korrnbloem' on the square, which has very unusual ceiling decoration!

Leave Langemarck by returning to the traffic lights and turning right and shortly pass the 20th Light Division Memorial on the right-hand side. Cross over the Steenbeek to reach **Cement House Cemetery**, which is still open for burials. Recently, as a result of building work near the canal, remains have been found and interred here. Further along the road is a small crossroads known as Iron Cross which can be identified by the Commonwealth War Graves Commission sign to **Ruisseau Farm Cemetery**. At the next crossroads turn left into Pilkemseweg and shortly left again and immediately right into Moortelweg (Admiral's Road). This area was part of the ground lost by the French on 22 April. There is a good view from Moortelweg across to Ypres. The next cemetery, **No Man's Cot**, was named after a small building which stood on the opposite of the road. It was used from July 1917 to March 1918. Where the road bends sharply to the right a track leads down to the new Turco Farm. Follow the road to the next crossroads. This point, known as Morteldje, was the furthest point reached by the Germans on the evening and night of 22 April 1915. Continue along Admiral's Road to pass the rebuilt Canadian and Hampshire Farms before reaching the small **Track 'X' Cemetery** on the left-hand side of the road. The site of this cemetery was between the Allied and German front lines in June 1917. Begun, following the advance, at the end of July 1917, it was only used until November of the same year. Shortly after passing Track 'X' Cemetery turn right into Hoge Ziekenweg (Buff's Road). The ground on either side of Buff's Road between here and New Irish Farm Cemetery was where the Lahore Division attacks took place **(See walk 1)**. On reaching New Irish Farm Cemetery, turn round and return to the junction with Admiral's Road. Continue across the crossroads to reach **Buff's Road Cemetery**. This cemetery was constructed by battalions of the Royal Sussex Regiment and the Royal Artillery. It was used between July 1917 and March 1918. After the Armistice it was enlarged by bringing in graves from smaller plots. One officer, killed in 1915, was brought here from Brielen churchyard. On leaving the cemetery the new Mouse Trap Farm can be seen on the left-hand side of the road. it was here that Captain Scrimger won his Victoria Cross. On reaching the main road, cross the N 38 to join the N 313 and follow the signs to Ypres (Centrum).

Total distance approximately 25 miles.

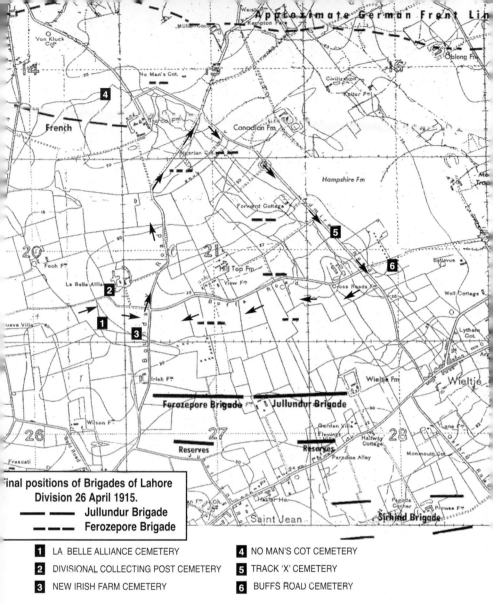

Final positions of Brigades of Lahore Division 26 April 1915.

——— · ——— Jullundur Brigade

——— —— —— Ferozepore Brigade

1	LA BELLE ALLIANCE CEMETERY	**4**	NO MAN'S COT CEMETERY
2	DIVISIONAL COLLECTING POST CEMETERY	**5**	TRACK 'X' CEMETERY
3	NEW IRISH FARM CEMETERY	**6**	BUFFS ROAD CEMETERY

MAP 19. BATTLEFIELD WALK NO. 1.

Walk No. 1: The Lahore Division attack area.

Map IGN No.2 Lille-Dunkerque   **Map 19.**

The ground around St. Jan and La Brique (De Brieke) has been developed for housing and light industry, so the battlefield is best seen from Buff's Road.

La Belle Alliance and Divisional Collecting Post Cemeteries.

Leave the Grote Markt by Korte Torhoutstraat, which runs to the left of the building at the end of the square beside the road to the Menin Gate, and turn left into Lange Torhoutstraat. Carry straight on past Commonwealth War Graves Commission signs, to the La Brique cemeteries, on the right-hand side. If you wish to visit the grave of Major Brodhurst, 1/4th Gurkha Rifles, he is buried in **La Brique Military Cemetery No 2**, the grave reference is Plot I, Row G, 21. Follow the main road through the industrial area to pass the Hotel Rabbit on the left. Go straight ahead at the next roundabout, towards a large red building, to reach traffic lights on the N 38. Cross the main road, signposted Pilckem, and after about 100 yards take the small road on the right, Hoge Ziekenweg (Buff's Road). There are Commonwealth War Graves Commission signs to **La Belle Alliance and Divisional Collecting Post Cemeteries**. The first of these cemeteries was started in February 1916 by units of the King's Royal Rifle Corps. It was only used for two months, in that year, but was in use again in July and August 1917. It was named after a farmhouse, which stood close by. The second was started by field ambulances of the 48th (South Midland) and 58th (London) Divisions in August 1917. In use until January 1918 it was much enlarged after the Armistice. After passing these two cemeteries turn right and park in front of **New Irish Farm**

New Irish Farm Cemetery.

Junction of Buff's Road and Admiral's Road. Buff's Road Cemetery can just be seen.

Cemetery. This cemetery was begun in August 1917, and used until November, and again in April and May 1918. It contained, at the Armistice, only seventy-three graves but now has almost five thousand. Among those buried here is Lieutenant-Colonel A G Burt, 1/York & Lancs, who was killed on 23 April 1915 **(See Chapter 2)**. The grave reference is Plot IV, Row E, 8.

When the Lahore Division carried out its attack on 26 April 1915 it did so from positions to the west of Wieltje, behind the modern main N 38 road over which you crossed just before turning into Buff's Road. The Jullundur Brigade was on the right and the Ferozepore Brigade on the left. The road on which you are parked was known as Boundary Road as it constituted the boundary between the French and British forces. As described in Chapter 2, the brigades moved out across the open ground towards Buff's Road, on past Hill Top Farm but then, when they breasted Hill Top ridge, were cut down by enemy fire. Leave your car at New Irish Farm Cemetery, cross over Buff's Road and walk up Boundary Road. As you do so Hill Top Farm and Hill Top ridge are on your right. The ground clearly drops away from Hill Top ridge and then rises again towards the German lines on Mauser ridge. One can only imagine the target that was given to the enemy as the two brigades appeared over the crest. The French attack was launched from positions well in advance of the Lahore Division, in the vicinity of Turco Farm, which is immediately in front. Follow the road to the crossroads and turn right into Mortelweg (Admiral's Road). There is a

Hampshire Farm and Track 'X' Cemetery from Admiral's Road.

Track 'X' Cemetery.

house nearby bearing Commonwealth War Graves Commission signs to **No Man's Cot** and **Minty Farm Cemeteries**. As you walk down Admiral's road you will pass the new Canadian and Hampshire Farms on the left-hand side. On the right are Forward Cottage and a farm building incorporating a blockhouse. **Track 'X' Cemetery** is on the left-hand side **(See Car Tour No. 2)**. As you go down the road, Buff's Road Cemetery comes into view on the left and also the 50th Division Memorial in front. Continue to the crossroads and turn right into Buff's Road. At the end of the attack on 26 April the brigades of the Lahore Division were in positions on either side of the road. It was in the ground between Boundary and Admiral's Road that Issy Smith and Mir Dast won their Victoria Crosses. As you progress along Buff's Road, towards New Irish Farm, the rise in the ground past Hill Top Farm and on to the ridge becomes very clear. One can also see the ground down towards the 50th Division Memorial and St. Jan from which the Division launched the attack. On reaching **New Irish Farm Cemetery** retrace your route to return to Ypres.

Walk No.2: Kitchener's Wood.

Map IGN No.2 Lille-Dunkerque   **Map 20.**

Drive from Ypres to St. Julien **(See Car tour No. 2)**. Park your car at **St Julien Dressing Station Cemetery** and walk back to the main road. Turn right towards St. Julien, cross over the road and turn left into a small road, Peperstraat. About two hundred yards along on the right-hand side note a small track between two houses. This is where you will emerge at the end of the walk. A further fifty yards will bring you

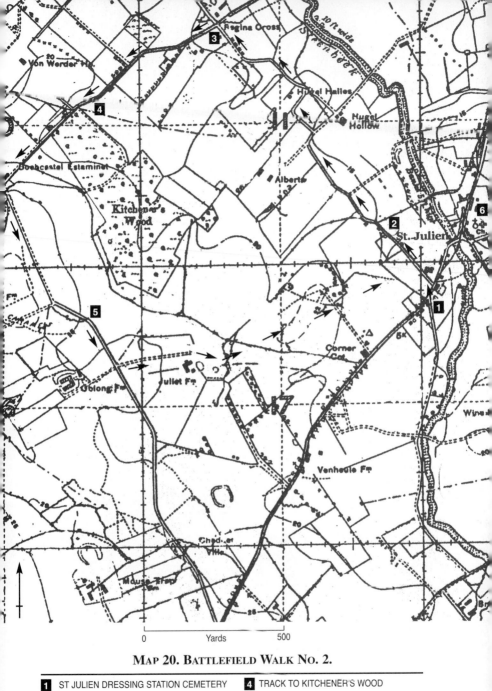

MAP 20. BATTLEFIELD WALK No. 2.

1	ST JULIEN DRESSING STATION CEMETERY		**4**	TRACK TO KITCHENER'S WOOD
2	COMMAND BUNKER		**5**	KITCHENER'S WOOD MEMORIAL
3	REGINA CROSS		**6**	ST JULIEN CHURCH

Command bunker in St. Julien.

to a large bunker, set back from the road on the right-hand side. This was a command bunker, but it is not the one known as 'Alberta', which was on the other side of the road and close to the edge of Kitchener's Wood. **(See map 20 page 121)** It was from the land behind the bunker that elements of the German 51st Reserve Division

Aerial view of Kitchener's Wood in 1917. IWM Q 43221

Kitchener's Wood memorial.

struck after the first gas attack. Carry on past a large white factory building and after several bends in the road reach a set of crossroads, Regina Cross. Turn left into Bruine Broekstraat and shortly pass a private road on the right. This road marks the approximate boundary between the German 51st and 52nd Reserve Divisions. A further two hundred yards will bring you to a track on the left, which was in existence in 1915. At that time it formed one edge of what was known in French as the Bois des Cuisiniers. It was the translation of this name into English that led to it being known as Kitchener's Wood. It was not named after the Secretary of State for War, Lord Kitchener. The boundary of the wood ran along the road for about one hundred and fifty yards. The further edge then ran, from the road, parallel with the

KITCHENER'S WOOD

20K.110
28.C.15d
11°
23-4-1

track before it widened out to extend for a further three hundred yards or so. If you go to the end of the track you can get some idea of the ground covered by the wood. Return to the road and walk beside what was the north-western edge of the wood. It ended about half way between the track and the next turning on the left, Wijngaardstraat. Take this road and after about five hundred yards there is a house on the left. Outside the house stands a new memorial, in the shape of a tree, commemorating Kitchener's Wood. Continue on the road to reach a small crossroads. To the right is Oblong Farm, which caused Lieutenant-Colonel Boyle such problems, **(See Chapter 2)** and to the left Juliet Farm. On the night of 22 April 1915 the front line ran from Oblong Farm to the road, just before the crossroads, then out in front of Kitchener's Wood and on to St. Julien, near the site of the bunker. Take the path down to Juliet Farm, which becomes a paved track once through the farm. It was from the ground in front, and to the right, of the farm that the Canadian 10th and 16th Battalions mounted the midnight attack on Kitchener's Wood on the night of 22/23 April. Note that the original site of Juliet Farm was on the other side of the track. Note also the bunkers in the farm grounds. Continue along the track and emerge between the two houses mentioned earlier. Walk back to St. Julien and return to Ypres. Whilst in St. Julien you may wish to visit the church and cemetery. It was from the cemetery that Lance Corporal Fisher started forward in the action that was to win him the Victoria Cross.

APPENDIX ONE

ORDER OF BATTLE: SECOND ARMY APRIL 1915

G.O.C General Sir Horace Smith-Dorrien.

Brigadier-General, General Staff Brigadier-General G T Forestier-Walker.

V Corps: Lieutenant-General Sir H C O Plumer.

Brigadier-General, General Staff Brigadier-General H S Jeudwine.

27th Division: Major-General T D'O Snow.

80th Brigade	81st Brigade	82nd Brigade
2/K.S.L.I.	1/Royal Scots.	1/Royal Irish.
3/K.R.R.C.	2/Gloucestershire.	2/D.C.L.I.
4/K.R.R.C.	2/Camerons.†	2/R.Irish Fus.
4/Rifle Brigade.	1/A. & S. H.	1/Leinster.
P.P.C.L.I.	9/Royal Scots.*	1/Cambridgeshire.*‡
	9/A. & S. H.*	

28th Division: Major-General E S Bulfin.

83rd Brigade	84th Brigade	85th Brigade
2/King's Own.	2/Northumberland Fus.†	2/Buffs.
2/E.Yorkshire.	1/Suffolk.	3/Royal Fus.
1/K.O.Y.L.I.	2/Cheshire.	2/E.Surrey.
1/York & Lancaster.	1/Welch.	3/Middlesex.
5/King's Own.*	12/London (Rangers).*	8/Middlesex.*
3/Monmouthshire.*	1/Monmouthshire.*	

* Attached Territorial Force units. † Lent to 5th Division. ‡ Four companies distributed between the Regular battalions.

Geddes's Detachment: Colonel A D Geddes.

Formed (without any staff) on 23 April 1915 of four battalions from 28th Division.

2/Buffs (less B Coy.), 3/Middlesex, 5/King's Own and 1/ York & Lancaster.

It was subsequently reinforced by another battalion from 28th Division – 2/East Yorkshire and two from 27th Division, 9/Royal Scots and 2/D.C.L.I.

1st Canadian Division: Lieutenant-General E A H Alderson.

1st Canadian Bde.	**2nd Canadian Bde.**	**3rd Canadian Bde.**
1st Battalion. *(Western Ontario Regt.).*	5th Battalion. *(Western Cavalry).*	13th Battalion. *(R. Highlanders of Canada).*
2nd Battalion. *(Eastern Ontario Regt.).*	7th Battalion. *(1st British Columbia Regt.).*	14th Battalion. *(R.Montreal Regt.).*
3rd Battalion. *(Toronto Regt.).*	8th Battalion. *(Winnipeg Rifles).*	15th Battalion. *(48th Highlanders of Canada).*
4th Battalion.	10th Battalion. *(10th Canadians).*	16th Battalion. *(Canadian Scottish).*

50th (1/Northumbrian) Division (T.F.): Major-General Sir W F L Lindsay.

149th Brigade *(1/Northumberland).*	**150th Brigade** *(1/York & Durham)*	**151st Brigade** *(1/Durham L.I.)*
4/Nrthd Fus.	4/E.Yorkshire.	6/Durham L.I.
5/Nrthd Fus.	4/Green Howards.	7/Durham L.I.
6/Nrthd Fus.	5/Green Howards.	8/Durham L.I.
7/Nrthd Fus.	5/Durham L.I.	9/Durham L.I.

4th Division: Major-General H F M Wilson.

10th Brigade	**11th Brigade**	**12th Brigade**
1/Royal Warwickshire.	1/Somerset L.I.	1/King's Own.
2/Seaforths.	1/E.Lancashire.	2/Royal Irish.
1/Royal Irish Fus.	1/Hampshire.	2/Lancashire Fus.
2/Royal Dublin Fus.	1/Rifle Brigade.	2/Essex.
7A & S.H.*	Ldn Rifle Brig.*	5/S.Lancs.*
		2/Monmouthshire *

Lahore Division: Major-General H D'U Keary.

Ferozepore Bde.	**Jullundur Bde.**	**Sirhind Bde.**
Connaught Rangers.	1/Manchester.	1/Highland L.I.
9th Bhopal Infantry.	40th Pathans.	15th Sikhs.
57th Wilde's Rifles.	47th Sikhs.	1/1st Gurkhas.
129th Baluchis.	59th Sceinde Rifles.	1/4th Gurkhas.
4/London.*	4/Suffolk.*	4/King's.*

* Attached Territorial Force Units.

Between 7.50 a.m. 28 April and 7 May 1915 the Second Army on the Ypres battle front was replaced by PLUMER'S FORCE: V Corps (2 Cavalry Division, 27th, 28th, 1st

Canadian and Lahore Divisions); together with the 10th and 11th Infantry Brigades (4th Division); 149th, 150th and 151st Infantry Brigades (50th Division); 13th Infantry Brigade (5th Division); and 54th and 55th Field Companies Royal Engineers (7th Division).

5th Division: Major-General T L N Morland.

13th Brigade	14th Brigade	15th Brigade
2/K.O.S.B.	1/Devonshire.	1/Norfolk.
2/D. of Wellington's	1/East Surrey.	1/Bedfordshire.
1/RoyalWest Kent.	1/D.C.L.I.	1/Cheshire.
2/K.O.Y.L.I.	2/Manchester.	1/Dorsetshire.
9/London.*	5/Cheshire.*	6/King's.*

* Attached Territorial Force Units.

APPENDIX TWO

Order of Battle: Détachement d'Armée de Belgique April 1915

Commander General Putz.

Composition on 20th April

Groupement de Nieuport: 38th Division & 81st Territorial Division
General Hély d'Oissel.

Groupment d'Elverdinghe: 45th Division & 87th Territorial Division
General Quinquandon.

23rd April: As above, plus the 153rd Division.

25th April: As above, plus the IX Corps (18th & 152nd Divisions).

18th Division: General Lefèvre (Justinien).

35th Brigade	36th Brigade
32nd Infantry Regt.	77th Infantry Regt.
66th Infantry Regt.	135th Infantry Regt.

45th Division: General Quinquandon.

90th Brigade	91st Brigade
2nd Zouaves de marche.	7th Zouaves de marche.
1st Tirailleurs de marche.	3rd Zouaves de marche.

152nd Division: General Joppé.

304th Brigade

268th Infantry Regt.
290th Infantry Regt.

4th Moroccan Brigade

1st Moroccan Infantry Regt.
8th Tirailleurs de marche.

153rd Division: General Deligny.

306th Brigade

418th Infantry Regt.
2nd & 4th Battalions
Chasseurs à pied.

3rd Moroccan Brigade

1st mixe Zouaves et
Tirailleurs.
9th Zouaves de marche.

87th Territorial Division: General Roy.

173rd Brigade

73rd Territorial Regt.
74th Territorial Regt.

174th Brigade

76th Territorial Regt.
79th Territorial Regt.
80th Territorial Regt.

186th Brigade

100th Territorial Regt.
102nd Territorial Regt.

APPENDIX THREE

Order of Battle: German Fourth Army April 1915

Commander: General Duke Albrecht von Württemberg.

Chief of Staff: Major-General Ilse.

XV Corps: General von Deimling.

30th Division.

60th Brigade
99th Regiment.
143rd Regiment.

85th Brigade
105th Regiment.
136th Regiment.

39th Division.

61st Brigade
126th Regiment.
132nd Regiment.

82nd Brigade
171st Regiment.
172nd Regiment.

XXII Reserve Corps: General von Falkenhayn.

43rd Reserve Division.

85th Reserve Bde.	86th Reserve Bde.
201st Reserve Regt.	203rd Reserve Regt.
202nd Reserve Regt.	204th Reserve Regt.
	15th Reserve Jäger Battalion.

44th Reserve Division.

207th Reserve Regiment (88th Reserve Brigade) only.

XXIII Reserve Corps: General von Rathen.

45th Reserve Division.

89th Reserve Bde.	**90th Reserve Bde.**
209th Reserve Regt.	210th Reserve Regt.
212th Reserve Regt.	211th Reserve Regt.
	17th Reserve Jäger Battalion.

46th Reserve Division.

91st Reserve Bde.	**92nd Reserve Bde.**
213rd Reserve Regt.	215th Reserve Regt.
214th Reserve Regt.	216th Reserve Regt.
	18th R.Jäger Battalion.

XXVI Reserve Corps: General von Hügel.

51st Reserve Division.

101st Reserve Bde.	**102nd Reserve Bde.**
233rd Reserve Regt.	235th Reserve Regt.
234th Reserve Regt.	236th Reserve Regt.
	23rd R. Jäger Battalion.

52nd Reserve Division.

103rd Reserve Bde.	**104th Reserve Bde.**
237th Reserve Regt.	239th Reserve Regt.
238th Reserve Regt.	240th Reserve Regt.
	24th R. Jäger Battalion.

Attached:
37th Landwehr Bde. (73rd & 74th Landwehr Regiments).
2nd Reserve Ersatz Bde. (3rd & 4th Reserve Ersatz Regiments).

XXVII Reserve Corps: General von Carlowitz.

53rd Reserve Division (Saxon).

105th Reserve Bde.

241st Reserve Regt.
242nd Reserve Regt.

106th Reserve Bde.

243rd Reserve Regt.
244th Reserve Regt.
25th R. Jäger Battalion.

Attached:
38th Landwehr Bde. (77th & 78th Landwehr Regiments).

54th Reserve Division (Württemberg).

107th Reserve Bde.

245th Reserve Regt.
246th Reserve Regt.

108th Reserve Bde.

247th Reserve Regt.
248th Reserve Regt.
28th R. Jäger Battalion.

Other Units

2nd Marine Bde.

2nd Marine Regt.

4th Marine Bde.

4th Marine Matrosen Regt.
5th Marine Matrosen Regt.

APPENDIX FOUR

The Ross Rifle

Just before the turn of the century, the Canadian Minister of Militia, Sir Frederick Borden, moved to induce the Birmingham Small Arms Co. (B.S.A.) to set up a plant in Canada, to manufacture Lee-Enfield rifles. Up until this time all Canadian Service equipment had been obtained from British sources with the inherent problem that, when supplies were needed in Canada, they were also needed in Britain. This failing was adequately demonstrated when, in 1900, the Canadian government placed a substantial order for rifles. No supplies were available as all factories in Britain were working to capacity to meet the needs of the South African campaign.

The bid to bring B.S.A. to Canada failed but in 1901 Sir Charles Ross approached the Canadian government with an offer to supply it with a .303 rifle. He claimed that the breech mechanism was new but in truth it was a modified Mannlicher system. In 1902, after some inconclusive tests, the Canadian government opted to accept the rifle even thought it meant departing from the principle of uniformity throughout Colonial and Imperial armies. As part of the deal it was agreed that construction would be carried out a plant to be built in Quebec. The initial order was for 1,000 rifles to be delivered in 1903. In the event the first completed order did not reach the Militia until 1905, although some were delivered in 1904 to the police and to other government bodies. The delay was put down to 'problems in production' but was certainly due, in part at least, to concern over the jamming experienced following multiple firing. The rifle produced, the Mark I, had a 28 inch barrel, weighed 7½ lbs. and had no provision for the attachment of a bayonet.

The Mark II, which went into production almost immediately, had more than seventy modifications, including changes to the firing and sighting mechanisms. Further modifications to the Mark II produced a series of starred models e.g. Mark II**. It was this model which attained fame as a 'target rifle' at Bisley but which still had major failings as a 'service rifle'. By the outbreak of war the Mark III had become the standard issue. The weight had gone up to 9½ lbs. the rifling had changed from right to left, and the length

Ross .303 Mark III rifle

131

of the barrel increased to 30½ inches. At all times, from its first acceptance, the Ross rifle was compared unfavourably with the Lee-Enfield rifle, the standard British issue. The problem experienced by the users of the Mark III rifle was still its tendency to jam on repeated fire. The fault was less marked when Canadian ammunition was used but was enhanced when standard issue British .303 ammunition, which was manufactured to lower specifications, was fired.

When the Canadians reached England and embarked on a training programme on Salisbury Plain, complaints increased. Back sights were easily damaged or even broken off, bayonets became detached when the rifle was fired, and jamming continued. Before going to France, Princess Patricia's Canadian Light Infantry, which was to be brigaded with British battalions, insisted on replacing the Ross rifles with Lee-Enfields. At the same time the Canadian Cavalry Commander argued that the length of the Ross rifle made it unsuitable as a cavalry weapon. This was accepted and Lee-Enfields issued instead.

When the Canadian 1st Division reached France in 1915 they found that their problems were accentuated. The length of the Ross rifle made movement difficult in the confines of a trench. The difficulties with the fragile sights and the bayonets also increased. If a bayonet flew off into No Man's Land it had to be retrieved, after dark, with the attendant risks. The rifle soon became unpopular with the artillery because the limber brackets, designed for the Lee-Enfield, failed to hold it securely, allowing the rifle to slip sideways and foul the wheel spokes. In spite of orders from Commanding Officers that possession of a Lee-Enfield rifle was not permitted, many men re-equipped themselves from British casualties. After Second Ypres the Canadian Divisional Commander requested his brigade and battalion commanders to report their experiences with the Ross rifle. Responses ranged from favourable to outright rejection but, significantly, adverse comments were received from General A W Currie, Lieutenant-Colonel L J Lipsett, and Lieutenant-Colonel F O W Loomis.

Following the reports Lieutenant-General Alderson recommended replacement of the rifle, but the political repercussions of such a move were unacceptable to the Canadian government. At this juncture Sir John French intervened and authorised the issue of Lee-Enfield rifles to the Canadian 1st Division. In a letter to Lord Kitchener he justified his action by saying that he intended shortly to employ the Canadians in a major offensive, and they must be capable of sustained fire. Given the shortage of Canadian ammunition and the lack of confidence expressed in the Ross rifle he had no alternative but to act as he did.

The authorities then turned their attention to the 2nd Division. This Division was already in England and preparing to go to France. All its rifles were re-chambered to the dimensions of the Lee-Enfield. This it was believed would mean that the problem with the ammunition would be erased. Unfortunately, this was not to be the case. The real problem lay in the action of the rifle. The straight pull through system of ejection of the empty case, could not achieve the unseating force of the Lee-Enfield's bolt lever acting on a screw thread. In the Spring of 1916 a copy of a letter sent from an American citizen serving as an officer at Shorncliffe was forwarded to Major-General W G Gwatkin the Chief of the General Staff in Ottawa. In the letter the writer stated that '85 per cent of men do not like the Ross rifle'. Asked by Major-General Gwatkin to comment on this and other extracts from the letter, General Alderson submitted a list of ten points in defence of the assertion. In turn his letter reached the Minister of Militia, Sir Sam Hughes, who issued an emphatic defence of the Ross rifle and at the same time censured Lieutenant-General Alderson. To compound the offence to Lieutenant-General Alderson he then ordered copies of his letter to be sent to all Canadian officers, down to battalion commanders, in England and France.

In respose to this remarkable behaviour Lieutenant-General Alderson organised a further poll, throughout the 2nd and 3rd Divisions, concerning the confidence of the men in the weapon. Armed with the replies to the questionnaire he then consulted the new Commander-in-Chief. Sir Douglas Haig, on seeing the results, recommended to the War Office, that both divisions should be rearmed. By mid-June all parties concerned had agreed to this recommendation and by late August the Ross rifle was withdrawn. The final act of this protracted drama, took place in September 1916 when the 4th Division was similarly rearmed.

Major-General Sir Sam Hughes, Canadian Minister of Militia.

Lee Enfield Mk III.

APPENDIX FIVE

Sir Horace Smith-Dorrien's letter to Sir John French 27 April 1915

Advanced Headquarters, 2nd Army
27th April 1915.

My dear Robertson,

In order to put the situation before the Commander-in-Chief, I propose to enter into a certain amount of detail.

You will remember that I told Colonel Montgomery [H. M. de F., General Staff, G.H.Q.] the night before last, after seeing General Putz's orders, that as he was only putting in a small proportion of his troops (and those at different points) to the actual attack, I did not anticipate any great results. You know what happened – the French right, instead of gaining ground, lost it, and the left of the Lahore Division did the same, but the British regiment on the right of the Lahore Division, the Manchesters, did very well and took some enemy trenches and held them for a considerable time.

The Northumberland Brigade to their right made a very fine attack on St. Julien and got into it, but were unable to remain there.

Away to the right, between St. Julien and our old trenches about square D.10 [85th Brigade area], there was a good deal of fighting, but with fairly satisfactory results – the Germans eventually retiring.

The enemy's losses were very heavy. Artillery observing officers claim to have mown them down over and over again during the day. At times, the fighting appears to have been heavy, and our casualties are by no means slight.

I enclose you on a separate paper the description of the line the troops are in at the moment. I saw General Putz last night about today's operations, and he told me he intends to resume the offensive with great vigour. I saw his orders, in which he claims to have captured Het Sas, but on my asking him what he meant he said the houses of that place which are to the west of the canal. He told me also that the success at Lizerne had been practically nil – in fact, that the Germans were still in possession of the village or were last night.

From General Putz's orders to-day, he is sending one brigade to cross the river east of Brielen to carry forward the troops on the east of the canal in the direction of Pilckem, and he assured me that this brigade was going to be pushed in with great vigour.

It was not till afterwards that I noticed that, to form his own reserve, he is withdrawing two battalions from the east of the canal and another two battalions from the front line in the same part to be used as a reserve on that bank of the river, so the net result of his orders is too send over six fresh battalions to the fighting line and to withdraw four which had already been employed.

I have lately received General Joppé's orders. He is the general commanding the attack towards Pilckem on the east of the canal, and I was horrified to see that he, instead of using the whole of this brigade across the canal for this offensive, is leaving one regiment back at Brielen, and only putting the other regiment across the canal to attack – so the net result of these latter orders with regard to the strength of the troops on the east of the canal for the fresh offensive is the addition of one battalion.

I need hardly say that I at once represented the matter pretty strongly to General Putz, but I want the Chief to know this as I do not think he must expect the French are going to do anything very great – in fact, although I have ordered the Lahore Division to co-operate when the French attack, at 1.15 p.m., I am pretty sure that our line to-night will not be in advance of where it is at the present time.

I fear the Lahore Division have had very heavy casualties, and so they tell me have the Northumbrians, and I am doubtful if it is worth losing any more men to regain this French ground unless the French do something really big.

Now, if you look at the map, you will see that the line the French and ourselves are now on allows the Germans to approach so close with their guns that the area east of Ypres will be very difficult to hold, chiefly because the roads approaching it from the west are swept by shell fire, and were all yesterday, and are being to-day. Again, they are now able to shell this place, Poperinghe, and have done it for the last three days; all day yesterday at intervals there were shells close to my Report Centre and splinters of one struck the house opposite in the middle of the day, and splinters of another actually struck the house itself about midnight – in other words, they will soon render this place unhealthy

If the French are not going to make a big push, the only line we can hold permanently and have a fair chance of keeping supplied, would be the G.H.Q. line passing just east of Wieltje and Potijze with a curved switch which is being prepared through Hooge, the centres of Squares I.18.d., I.24.b. and d. [that is by Hooge and Sanctuary Wood], to join on to our present line about a thousand yards north-east of Hill 60.

This, of course, means the surrendering of a great deal of trench line, but any intermediate line, short of that, will be extremely difficult to hold, owing to the loss of the ridge to the east of Zonnebeke, which any withdrawal must entail.

I think it right to put these views before the Chief, but at the same time to make it clear that, although I am preparing for the worst, I do not think we have arrived at the time when it is necessary to adopt these measures. In any case, a withdrawal to that line in one fell swoop would be almost impossible on account of the enormous amount of guns and paraphernalia which will have to be withdrawn first, and therefore, if withdrawal becomes necessary, the first contraction would be, starting from the left, our present line as far as the spot where the Haanebeke stream crosses the road at the junction of Squares D.7 and D.13 [1,500 yards east of St. Julien], thence along the subsidiary line which is already prepared, as far as the south-east corner of Square J.2 [1,500 yards south-east of Frezenberg, from whence a switch has been prepared into our old line on the east side of J.14.b., i.e. just excluding the Polygon Wood. I intend to-night if nothing special happens to re-organise the new front and to withdraw superfluous troops West of Ypres.

I always have to contemplate the possibility of the Germans gaining ground west of Lizerne, and this, of course, would make the situation more impossible – in fact, it all comes down to this, that unless the French do something really vigorous the situation might become such as to make it impossible for us to hold any line east of Ypres.

It is very difficult to put a subject such as this in a letter without appearing pessimistic – I am not in the least, but as an Army Commander I have of course to provide for every eventuality and I think it right to let the Chief know what is running in my mind.

More British troops, of course, could restore the situation – but I consider it to be out of the question, as it would interfere with a big offensive elsewhere which is after all the crux of the situation and will do more to relieve this situation than anything else.

Since writing above, our Cavalry report that the French actually took the whole of Lizerne last night capturing 120 Germans and are now attacking the bridgehead covering the bridge leading over the canal to Steenstraat.

General Putz has answered my protest and has ordered General Joppé to put in the whole of the fresh Brigade and not to leave one Regiment of it in reserve at Brielen. The attack is to commence at 1.15 p.m. and we are to assist with heavy artillery fire, and the Lahore Division is only to advance if they see the French troops getting on.

Our Cavalry is where it was last night, one division west of Lizerne, one dismounted in reserve holding G.H.Q. trenches east of Ypres, one dismounted in huts at Vlamertinghe.

I am still at my Advanced Headquarters in Poperinghe. Whether I remain here to-night again I do not know, the main advantage of my being here is my close touch with General Putz and my being able to impress my views upon him.

Yours sincerely,
H. L. Smith-Dorrien.

APPENDIX SIX

Background and burial/commemoration details of some officers mentioned in the text

Lieutenant-Colonel A P D Birchall

Arthur Percival Dearman Birchall was born in the county of Gloucestershire on 7 March 1877. He was educated at Eton and Magdalen College Oxford, and with a University Commission was gazetted, Second Lieutenant in the Royal Fusiliers (City of London Regiment), 23 May 1900. He joined the newly formed 4th Battalion of the Royal Fusiliers in South Africa, and for the next fifteen years was to serve with distinction. He was among the officers responsible for raising the new unit to the high level of the older battalions. From March 1904 to March 1907 he was Adjutant of the Royal Fusiliers. In April 1910 he was seconded to serve with the Royal Canadian Regiment, one of only two officers from the whole British Army to be so selected. In August 1914, his health having broken down under the rigours of the Canadian climate, he returned to England. Prevented by his medical condition from active service, he used his convalescence to produce a manual for use in the rapid training of a company for war. He returned to Canada in November and acted as Staff Captain to the 1st Brigade. He was appointed Colonel of the 4th Battalion in February 1915. He was killed in action on 24 April 1915.

In a Canadian record of the events leading up to the death of Lieutenant-Colonel Birchall he is described as leading his men forward 'carrying, after an old fashion, a light cane'. He cheerfully rallied his men, and, at the very moment when his example had infected them, fell dead at the head of his battalion. Lieutenant-Colonel Birchall has no known grave but is commemorated on the Menin Gate Memorial to the Missing, Ypres, Panel 6 and 8.

Captain J F C Dalmahoy

The son of Major-General Patrick Carfrae Dalmahoy, John Francis Cecil Dalmahoy was born on 25 February 1881. He was educated in Edinburgh and the Royal Military Academy, Sandhurst. He joined the Indian Army in January 1901 and by 1910 had been promoted to the rank of Captain. Initially attached to the King's Royal Rifles and for a short time with the 18th Bengal Lancers, he was posted to the 40th Pathans in 1902. When war was declared his regiment was in Hong Kong but was quickly transferred to France, where it landed in April 1915. During the attack by the 40th Pathans on 26 April Captain Dalmahoy was badly wounded, and advised to retire, but insisted in leading his men forward until killed by a burst of machine-gun fire.

Captain Dalmahoy is commemorated on Special Memorial No. 31 in New Irish Farm Cemetery, Ypres.

Captain B Farrell

Born in Kingston upon Hull, Yorkshire, on 28 June 1881, Bede Farrell was the eldest son of Thomas Farrell, Registrar of the Hull County Court. After attending Hymer's College, Hull, he qualified and became a practising solicitor in his home town in 1904. However, he had already been granted, in 1900, a commission in the 4th Territorial Battalion of the East Yorkshire Regiment. Following his attendance at a 'Course for Militia Infantry and Rifle Volunteers' in 1901 he was offered a commission in the Regular Army, but due to his legal studies was unable to accept. At the onset of war he immediately volunteered and served in Belgium from April 1915. He was killed on Saturday, 24 April, as the remnants of the battalion returned to the trenches.

Captain Farrell has no known grave but is commemorated on the Menin Gate Memorial to the Missing, Ypres, Panels 21 and 31.

Colonel A D Geddes

Augustus David Geddes was born into a military family, at Dover in Kent, on 6 June 1866. His father, Colonel John Geddes, had served with the 44th and 76th Regiments. After school in Cheltenham, he attended the Royal Military Academy, Sandhurst and was gazetted to the 2nd Battalion (The Buffs) East Kent Regiment, in February 1887. He served in the South African War, 1899-1901 and then passed Staff College in December 1903. After various appointments, including one as Staff Captain in the Intelligence Department at the War Office, he was promoted to the rank of Lieutenant-Colonel in February 1911 and to Colonel in February 1915. During the Second Battle of Ypres he commanded the Geddes's Detachment and was killed on 28 April 1915. He had closed down his headquarters on the previous night and set off, to return to Potijze. He spent the night at 13th Brigade headquarters and was unluckily killed when a shell burst in the room, as he was on the point of leaving.

Colonel Geddes is buried in Ypres Reservoir Cemetery. The grave reference is Plot IV, Row C, 4.

Lieutenant-Colonel W F R Hart-McHarg

William Frederick Richard Hart-McHarg was the only son of Major William Hart-McHarg of the 44th Regiment. Born on 16 February 1869 he moved to Canada in 1885 and qualified as a Barrister-at-Law and Solicitor of the Supreme Court of British Columbia, practising at Vancouver. He joined the Canadian Militia as a private, but rose to command the 7th Regiment and served for over twenty years. He went to the war in South Africa (1900-1902), with the first contingent, and was awarded the Queen's medal with four clasps.

Colonel Hart-McHarg was well known as a marksman. He shot for Canada on a number of occasions and was a member of the Canadian team at Bisley in 1907, 1910 and 1914. When war was declared in 1914 he was again among the first contingent to leave Canada, this time as Commanding Officer of the 7th Battalion. As recorded in Chapter Two he died on 24 April of wounds received the previous day. He is buried in Poperinghe Old Military Cemetery. The grave reference is Plot II, Row M, 3.

Also buried in Poperinghe Old Military Cemetery is Lieutenant-Colonel R L Boyle (10th Battalion Canadian Infantry) who died on the same day. His grave reference is Plot II, Row M, 54.

Brigadier-General J Hasler

Julian Hasler was born in Chichester, Sussex, on 16 October 1868. He was educated at Winchester College before entering the Royal Military Academy, Sandhurst. He was gazetted Second Lieutenant in the 3rd Battalion (The Buffs) East Kent Regiment on 19 September 1888. During the next twenty six years he served in many parts of the Empire, including South and West Africa and the northwest frontier of India. During the South African War he raised and commanded Hasler's Australian Scouts. After the outbreak of the European war he was promoted to the rank of Brigadier-General in February 1915 and given command of the 11th Infantry Brigade. He still held this post when he was killed, in St. Jean, when a shell hit his headquarters on 26 April. He was twice mentioned in Despatches by Sir John French, first in February 1915 and again, after his death, in June 1915.

Brigadier-General Hasler is buried in White House Cemetery, St. Jean, Ypres. The grave reference is Plot III, Row A, 5.

Lieutenant-Colonel H W E Hitchens

Henry William Ernest Hitchens also came from a family with strong military traditions. His father was a Major-General and his grand-father a Lieutenant-General. Born in May 1865, educated privately and at the Royal Military Academy, Sandhurst, he was gazetted Second Lieutenant in the 1st Battalion Manchester Regiment, on 25 August 1886. By 1895 he had reached the rank of Captain and been singled out as a soldier with good powers of organisation. He spent four years, from 1897, as adjutant of the Territorial Battalion before, in 1901, obtaining his Majority, a rank he was to hold for almost fourteen years. The 1st Manchester was sent to India in 1906, where Major Hitchens, now back with his old battalion, was present at the Great Coronation Durbar. In 1914 Major Hitchens was in temporary command of the battalion and thus responsible for bringing it, as part of the Lahore Division, back to Europe. Actively involved, again as temporary commander, in the fighting at Givenchy in December of that year, he received much praise for the quality of his leadership. Having received a leg wound in the Givenchy fighting, he was out of the line until April 1915. He rejoined his regiment and was killed in the Lahore Division attack on 26 April. Two days, before his death he had been promoted to Lieutenant-Colonel and given command of the battalion. Following his death a Military Memorial Service was accorded to Lieutenant-Colonel Hitchens at the depot of his regiment at Ashton-under-Lyne. He was also praised by General Sir Horace Smith-Dorrien and General Sir James Wilcocks, commander of the Indian Army

Corps, for the quality of his leadership and the steadfastness of his battalion 'the gallant Manchesters'.

Lieutenant-Colonel Hitchens is buried in White House Cemetery, St. Jean, Ypres. The grave reference is Plot III, Row A, 1.

Brigadier-General J F Riddell

James Foster Riddell, the only son of John Riddell, of the family of Riddell, formerly of Riddell in Roxburghshire, was born on 17 October 1861. He was educated at Wellington and the Royal Military Academy, Sandhurst and gazetted Second Lieutenant in the Northumberland Fusiliers in July 1881. He served in the Hazara Campaign of 1888 and in the South African War 1899 – 1902. During the latter war he raised, and later commanded, the 3rd Battalion of the Northumberland Fusiliers. At the end of the war, the Battalion was disbanded and, he succeeded to the command of the 2nd Battalion. He remained in this post until, in 1911, he was appointed Brigade Commander of the Northumberland Infantry Brigade. When war was declared he was promoted to the rank of Brigadier-General and made responsible for the coastal defences in the area around Newcastle. At the same time he remained in command of Brigade and prepared it for war. The Brigade crossed to France in mid-April and as a result of the gas attack, on 22 April, was rushed to the front. Brigadier-General Riddell was killed, within a week of reaching France, on 26 April 1915.

Brigadier-General Riddell is buried in Tyne Cot Cemetery, Zonnebeke. The grave reference is Plot XXXIV, Row H, 14.

Lieutenant-Colonel E W R Stephenson

Ernest William Rokeby Stephenson was born on 4 August 1864. He was gazetted Second Lieutenant in the Middlesex Regiment on 23 August 1884. He served as Adjutant to the Regiment from August 1890 to August 1894 and again from April 1900 to December 1901. Posted to South Africa in 1902 he subsequently saw service in Hong Kong (1906) and Singapore in 1908. He was promoted to the rank of Lieutenant-Colonel in February 1912, whilst in India, where he remained until war broke out.

He has no known grave but is commemorated on the Menin Gate Memorial to the Missing, Ypres, Panel 49 and 51.

Private E Rust

Private Edward Rust does not feature in the narrative but he served with the 4/Green Howards (Yorkshire Regiment). Private Rust was the son of the Reverend Edward Rust, Vicar of Hamsteels County Durham. He was educated at Scorton Grammar School in Yorkshire and enlisted at Catterick. He died on 30 April 1915 and is buried in Hazebrouck Communal Cemetery. The grave reference is Plot I, Row G, 35. He was only one of the many who died in April and May 1915 but he must have been a remarkable young man. His grave is marked by a stone which bears the following inscription:

1830 Private
Edward Rust
Yorkshire Regiment

30th April 1915

Seriously wounded while
advancing with his regiment
in the fighting near
St. Julien Saturday 24 April 1915
he was taken to the Field
Hospital but was so eager to
uphold the honour of his
regiment and to serve his
country that he returned next
day to the firing line and
remained with his comrades
until they were relieved and
died on April 30th courageous
to the end and beloved by
all who knew him.

FURTHER READING

1. *Official History of the War. Military Operations in France & Belgium, 1915.*
Volume I. Brigadier-General J E Edmonds and Captain G C Wynne. Macmillan
1927.
2. *Official History of the Canadian Army in the First World War. Canadian
Expeditionary Force 1914-1919.* Colonel G W L Nicholson. The Queen's
printer Ottawa 1962.
3. *The Fiftieth Division 1914-1919.* Everard Wyrall. Reprinted by the Naval &
Military Press 1999.
4. *Gas! The Battle for Ypres, 1915.* T J L McWilliams and R James Steel.
Vanwell Publishing Ltd. Ontario 1985.
5. *The Poisonous Cloud. Chemical Warfare in the First World War.* L F Haber.
Clarendon Press. Oxford 1986.
6. *VCs of the First World War. The Western Front 1915.* P Batchelor & C
Matson. Sutton Publishing 1997.
7. *Welcome to Flanders Fields.* D G Dancocks. McClelland and Stewart.
Toronto 1988.
8. *Major & Mrs Holt's Battlefield Guide to the Ypres Salient.* Tonie and Valmai
Holt. Updated version Pen & Sword Books Ltd. 1999.
9. *Before Endeavours Fade.* A Guide to the Battlefields of the First World War.
Rose Coombs MBE. Updated version 'After the Battle' Publications.
10. Other volumes in the *Battleground Europe Series*, particularly: *Walking the
Salient* by Paul Reed and *Passchendaele* by Nigel Cave.

Selective Index

Allen, Lieutenant-Colonel J.W., 80
Admiral's Road, 49, 80, 119,120
Alberta, 49, 122
Alderson, Lieutenant-General E.A.H., 30, 36, 38, 40, 41, 50, 62, 63, 64, 66, 72, 86
Anderson, Lieutenant-Colonel W.C., 80
BEF, 17, 19
Bell, Lieutenant-Colonel M.H.L., 62, 65
Bellew, Lieutenant E.D., 63, 96, 97, 115
Berlin Wood, 30, 31, 69, 72, 89, 90, 103
Binding, Rudolph, 67, 83
Birchall, Lieutenant-Colonel A. P., 51, 54, 137
Blair, Lieutenant-Colonel A. S., 51
Boer War, 27
Boesinghe, 33, 35, 73
Bombarded Cross Roads, 39, 64, 65, 113
Bonaparte, Napoleon, 107
Boundary Road, 74
Boyle, Lieutenant-Colonel R. L., 45, 46, 124
Brielen, 31, 40, 45, 89
Brielen bridge, 42, 43, 54
Brodhurst, Major B. M. L., 80
Buff's Road, 75, 118, 119, 120
Bulfin, Major-General E. S., 32, 69, 70
Burland, Lieutenant-Colonel W.W., 63
Burt, Lieutenant-Colonel A. G., 53, 119
Bush, Brigadier-General J. E., 62
Cassel, 12, 13, 51, 86
Cavendish, Lieutenant-Colonel Lord R. F., 50
Cemeteries:
    Artillery Wood, 110
    Bard Cottage, 108
    Buff's Road, 116
    Cement House, 116
    Divisional Collecting Post, 118
    Essex Farm, 107
    Grootebeek British, Reninghelst, 103
    Hazebrouck Comm., 75, 140
    La Belle Alliance, 118
    La Brique Military, No. 2, 118
    Langemarck (German), 116
    New Irish Farm, 118, 119
    No Man's Cot, 116
    Oxford Road, 112
    Poperinghe Old Military, 46, 55
    Potijze Chateau Grounds, 112
    Potijze Chateau Lawn, 112
    Potijze Chateau Wood, 112
    Potijze Burial Ground, 112
    Seaforth, Cheddar Villa, 112
    St. Julien Dressing Station, 113, 120
    Talana Farm, 108
    Track 'X', 116,119, 120
    Tyne Cot, 78, 114
    Wieltje Farm, 112
    Ypres Reservoir, 106
    Ypres Town, 112
Chateau des Trois Tours, 30, 106
Chlorine, 34, 37, 57, 89, 103
Colne Valley, 54
Currie, Brigadier-General A. W., 39, 42, 60, 63
Dalmahoy, Captain J. F. C., 75, 137
Egerton, Brigadier-General R. G., 72
Enfiladed Cross Roads, 63, 98, 113
Falkenhayn, Lieutenant-General E.von, 33
Farms:
    Boetleer's, 39, 64, 66, 69, 72, 98
    Burnt, 42
    Canadian, 74, 80, 81, 120
    Hampshire, 38, 41, 54, 119, 120
    Hill Top, 100, 120
    Juliet, 124
    Mouse Trap, 37, 41, 45, 47, 67, 69, 87, 99, 103, 116
    Oblong, 46, 124
    Spree, 39
    Turco, 74, 89, 90, 103, 116, 119
    Vanheule, 68, 78
    Zwaanhof, South, 54, 110
Farrell, Captain B., 65, 137
Fisher, Corporal F., 38, 95, 96, 114, 124
Foch, Maréchal F., 40, 51, 53, 66, 86, 89
Fortuin, 57, 62, 64, 65, 67, 68, 70
French, Field-Marshal Sir J., 18, 21, 22, 30, 35, 51, 53, 66, 70, 79, 82, 86, 88, 91, 92
Frezenberg ridge, 43, 87
Geddes, Colonel A. D., 50, 51, 52, 86, 106, 138
Geddes's Detachment, 50, 69
G.H.Q. Line, 24, 37, 38, 41, 60, 62, 64, 68, 76
Guynemeyer, G., 115
Haber, Fritz, 26
Haig, General Sir D., 18, 78, 92
Hall, Company-Sergeant Major F. W., 64, 97, 98, 99, 114
Hart-McHarg, Lieutenant-Colonel W. F. R., 54, 55, 138
Hasler, Brigadier-General J., 69, 70, 139
Hazebrouck, 75, 88, 140
Het Sas, 33, 44, 55, 87
Hicks, Lieutenant-Colonel F. R., 70
Hill, Colonel F. W., 51
Hill 60, 33, 35, 41, 86, 87
Hill Top ridge, 88, 100
Hitchens, Lieutenant-Colonel H. W. E., 74, 139
Hughes, Lieutenant-Colonel G. B., 42
Hull, Brigadier-General C. P. A., 54, 67, 68, 69
Ingalls, Private A. G., 23
Jaeger, August, 27, 28, 29
Jeudine, Brigadier-General H. S., 28
Joffre, General F., 18, 21, 89
Johnson, Major A. V., 65
Joppé, General, 72, 73, 87
Keary, Major-General H. D'U., 69
Keerselare, 35, 38, 96
King, Major W. B., 38, 95
Kitchener, Field-Marshall Lord H., 35, 92, 123

Kitchener's Wood, 44, 45, 48, 50, 51, 52, 54, 60, 63, 67, 68, 71, 72, 76, 122
Langemarck, 33, 34, 35, 44
Leckie, Lieutenant-Colonel R. G. E., 46
Lipsett, Lieutenant-Colonel L., 60, 98
Lizerne, 33, 44, 52, 55, 66, 81, 87
Locality C, 39, 42, 60, 62, 63, 89, 98, 114
Lynn, Private J., 89, 103
MacLaren, Major J., 47
Mathews, Major H. H., 23, 58
Mauser Ridge, 41, 44, 119
McCrae, J., 107
Mir Dast, Jemadar, 76, 101, 102, 120
Memorials:
    Brooding Soldier, Vancouver Corner, 114
    'Carrefour de la Rose', 110
    French Grenadier, 108
    Georges Guynemer, 115
    Kitchener's Wood, 122, 124
    New Zealand, 113, 114
    Troisième Regiment de Ligne, 108
    Steenstraat, 109
    50th Division, 112, 120
Mercer, Brigadier-General M, S., 51
Military Units: British:
Armies:
    First, 18, 78
    Second, 22, 40, 51, 66, 70, 81
Corps:
    II, 18
    III, 18
    V, 28, 30, 40, 42, 55, 70, 85
Divisions:
    4th, 51, 88, 89
    5th, 25, 64
    7th, 18
    27th, 22, 25, 28, 32, 42, 51, 62, 63, 70, 86, 89
    28th, 22, 25, 28, 30, 32, 40, 41, 51, 64, 66, 86
    29th, 21
    46th, 21
    50th, 51, 84
Brigades:
    10th, 54, 67, 68, 71, 86
    11th, 69, 70, 88, 89
    12th, 88, 89
    13th, 52, 54, 64, 86, 88
    80th, 33, 42
    81st, 33
    82nd, 33
    83rd, 32
    84th, 32
    85th, 32, 70
    149th, 51, 69, 70, 71, 76, 86
    150th, 51, 62, 63, 88
    151st, 51, 88
Battalions:
    7/A.& S.H., 68, 72, 76, 90
    2/Buffs, 41, 42, 43, 50, 54, 60, 62
    2/Chesire, 43, 64, 66

Connaught Rangers, 73, 76
2/D.C.L.I., 51, 52, 81
5/D.C.L.I., 68
2/ Duke of Wellington's, 53, 81
2/East Yorks., 40, 51, 52
4/East Yorks., 62
4/Green Howards, 62, 64
5/Green Howards, 69
1/Hampshire, 70
2/K.S.L.I., 42
2/K.O.Y.L.I., 53, 64, 69
2/K.O.S.B., 52, 53
5/King's Own, 41, 42, 50, 51, 52, 53, 81
2/Lancashire Fusiliers, 89, 103
4/London, 73, 80
9/London (Queen Victoria's Rifles), 53,64,69
12/London (Rangers), 64
1/Manchester, 71, 73, 74, 100
3/Middlesex, 41, 50, 51, 53, 54
8/Middlesex, 64, 65, 66
1/Monmouths., 43, 64, 66
2/Northumberland Fusiliers, 66
4/Northumberland Fusiliers, 69
7/Northumberland Fusiliers, 69
4/Rifle Brigade, 42, 54, 69
2/Royal Dublin Fusiliers, 68
3/Royal Fusiliers, 69, 70
1/Royal Irish Rifles, 64, 65, 68, 69
9/Royal Scots., 51, 52
1/Royal West Kent, 52
1/Royal Warwicks., 68
2/Seaforth Highlanders, 68
5/South Lancs., 90
1/Suffolk, 64, 66
4/Suffolk, 73
1/York & Lancaster, 42, 50, 51, 52, 53, 81
Military Units: Canadian:
Divisions:
    1st, 221, 22, 25, 29, 30, 35, 45
Brigades:
    1st, 40, 51
    2nd, 31, 38, 69
    3rd, 31, 37, 40, 42, 50, 51, 64
Battalions:
    1st, 53, 54, 68, 70
    2nd, 40, 47, 60, 61, 62, 64, 70
    3rd, 40, 47, 48, 62
    4th, 53, 54, 64, 68
    5th, 31, 70
    7th, 31, 38, 41, 42, 54, 60, 64
    8th, 31, 57, 58, 60, 62, 63, 70, 78
    10th, 31, 38, 45, 46, 60, 98
    13th, 31, 37, 38, 41, 43, 54, 60, 62
    14th, 31, 37, 38, 41, 60, 62, 64, 99
    15th, 31, 37, 38, 41, 57, 60, 62, 64
    16th, 31, 39, 42, 45, 60
    10th Battery Canadian Field Artillery, 38, 41, 45, 47, 114
    122nd Heavy Battery, 62

Military Units: French:
Divisions:
  45th Algerian, 22, 35, 41, 52
  87th Territorial, 22, 24, 25
  152nd, 72, 73
Brigades:
  80th Territorial, 66
Battalions:
  4th Chasseurs, 27
  1/1st Tiralilleurs, 37, 41, 43
  Zouaves, 37, 38, 51, 66
Military Units: German:
Corps:
  XV, 25
  XXII Reserve, 25
  XXIII Reserve, 25, 55
  XXVI Reserve, 25, 26, 31, 33, 57, 69, 72
  XXVII Reserve, 25, 31, 57
Brigades:
  2nd Reserve Ersatz, 25, 57
  37th Landwehr, 26, 44
  38th Landwehr, 25
  4th Marine, 57
Divisions:
  30th, 25
  39th, 25
  43rd Reserve, 26
  45th Reserve, 25, 33, 44
  46th Reserve, 25, 33, 44
  51st Reserve, 25, 34, 45, 57, 68, 89, 122
  52nd Reserve, 25, 33, 44, 72
  53rd Reserve, 25, 89
  54th Reserve, 25
Military Units: Indian:
Divisions:
  Lahore, 51, 69, 70, 71, 73, 74, 80, 81, 89, 119
Brigades:
  Ferozepore, 71, 74, 76, 78, 80, 119
  Jullundur, 71, 74, 76, 78, 119
  Sirhind, 71, 78, 80, 87, 88, 89
Battalions:
  129th Baluchis, 73, 76
  9th Bhopal Infantry, 73, 80
  1/1st Gurkhas, 80
  1/4th Gurkhas, 80
  40th Pathans, 71, 73, 74, 75
  57th Wilde's Rifles, 73, 76, 101
  59th Sceinde Rifles, 73
  47th Sikhs, 73, 75
Mordacq, Colonel, 51, 66, 72
Moulton-Barrett, Major E. M., 66
Neale, Major G.H., 43
Odlum, Major V. W., 54, 55, 63
Ormond, Major D. M., 46, 60, 64, 98
Perceval, Major-General E. M., 82
Perkins, Major A. C., 75
Pilckem, 33, 34, 44, 52, 72, 87
Pixley, Captain J., 110
Plumer, Lieutenant-General Sir H. C., 22, 30,

40, 63, 66, 69, 71, 86, 87, 88, 89, 92
'Plumer's Force', 83, 85, 89
Poelcappelle, 29, 115
Point 37, 70
Polygon Wood, 332, 33
Poperinghe, 30, 47, 51
Potijze, 32, 35, 42, 63, 65
Potijze chateau, 32, 62
Power, Major R. E., 50
Putz, General, 22, 27, 40, 52, 66, 70, 72, 80
Quiquandon, General, 22, 41, 43, 55, 70, 72,
  73, 87, 88
Reigersburg chateau, 106
Rennick, Lieutenant-Colonel F. R., 75
Rennie, Lieutenant-Colonel R., 48
Riddell, Brigadier-General J. F., 71, 72, 78, 140
Robertson, Lieutenant-General Sir W., 66, 81,82
Romer, Colonel C. F., 64
Ross rifle, 131, 132, 133
Rust, Private E., 140
St. Jean, 31, 41, 42, 70, 72
St. Julien, 31, 57, 62, 65, 67, 68, 88, 96, 122
St. Julien church, 45, 124
Salvation Corner, 110
Scott, Canon F. G., 48
Scrimger, Captain F. A. C., 99, 100 116
Smith, Corporal I., 74, 100, 101, 120
Smith-Dorrien, General Sir H., 27, 35, 40, 51,
  54, 66, 70, 79, 80, 81, 82, 85, 91, 92
Snow, Major-General T. D'O., 323, 35, 42, 63, 64
Stairs, Lieutenant G. W., 38, 95
Steenstraat, 29, 33, 35, 44, 52, 81, 87
Stephenson, Lieutenant-Colonel E. W. R., 42,
  54, 140
Strickland, Brigadier-General E. P., 71
Strudwick, Private V. J., 107
Turner, Brigadier-General R. E. W., 37, 39, 42,
  43, 45, 60, 62, 63
Tuson, Lieutenant-Colonel H. D., 51, 52, 81
Vlamertinghe, 31, 47, 51, 71
Walker, Brigadier-General W. G., 71, 80
Wallace, Lieutenant-Colonel W. B., 64
Wanless O'Gowan, Brigadier-General R., 52,
  53, 69
Watson, Lieutenant-Colonel D., 47
Wieltje, 24, 38, 50, 51, 62, 68, 70,119
Württemberg, General-Colonel Duke A. of, 26, 69
Zillebeke, 24, 29

144